# Rollercoaster of Hope

**Dhimant Bakshi** is the CEO of Imagicaaworld Entertainment Ltd. An INSEAD alumnus, he has also worked with Reliance Retail, Shoppers Stop, Future Group and Globus in a career spanning three decades. He is an advisory board member with Antarang foundation, creating a platform for an equitable future for the youth.

Dhimant actively mentors companies facing challenging situations, providing guidance in turnarounds and growth. He is also a sounding board for culture building for start-ups. He believes in happiness and creating delightful memories, both professionally and personally.

**Mayuresh Kore** is the CFO of Imagicaaworld Entertainment Ltd. In a career spanning twenty-three years, he has worked in investment banking, entrepreneurship, new businesses and corporate finance. He has interests in media and entertainment, hospitality and real estate, having run a project to develop a six-storey building on ancestral land in Mumbai first hand.

An avid cricketer, he has managed a legacy Mumbai Cricket Association (MCA) affiliated club for the last two decades and hopes that he can play competitive cricket for few more years!

## Praise for *Rollercoaster of Hope*

'We rarely see professionals staying to handle a bankruptcy situation when the business is a promoter-driven listed entity. What is interesting is two professionals, a new CEO and CFO, take on the onus of turnaround in a difficult situation and come out as a winner. The company is in an industry which is not very big, does not have history in the industry to learn. This is a fabulous example of ownership. I reiterate ownership is not by shareholding but by owning the situation. Readers will not find a better example of ownership than reading this book.'

**—B.S. Nagesh, Founder, TRRAIN, Former Chairman, Shoppers' Stop**

'I was always fascinated by the business of amusement parks. Their running is no less than a rollercoaster. In our country, the challenges and opportunities make it even more thrilling. Having tracked Imagicaa as both a customer and a business journalist through multiple cycles and ownership changes, I can surely say—the story has as many ups and downs as their rides.

I'm glad that Dhimant and Mayuresh have taken it upon themselves to tell this story to everyone. They're best placed to do so, because they know both the joy of seeing their guests and shareholders smile after a day at the park and the pains it took to keep the park up and running through the years.'

**—Mangalam Maloo, Senior Business News Anchor & Consumer Sector Expert**

'Dhimant Bakshi and Mayuresh Kore have taken a complex topic and turned it into an easy-to-understand narrative. This is the one of the best-written Indian turnaround stories that I have come across in recent years.'

**—Saurabh Mukherjea, Marcellus Investment Managers**

'This gripping account of Imagicaa's bankruptcy and revival offers investors invaluable real-world insights into distressed asset opportunities. The authors' honest portrayal of stakeholder dynamics, management challenges and the bankruptcy process provides a masterclass in crisis navigation rarely found in academic texts. From identifying red flags to recognising turnaround potential, this book equips investors with practical knowledge for evaluating distressed situations. A compelling blend of cautionary tale and success story that every serious investor should study.'

**—Vinay Paharia, Chief Investment Officer,**
**PGIM India MF**

'This book offers an honest and unvarnished look at what it truly takes to steer a company through financial distress and an NCLT process. The authors, Dhimant Bakshi and Mayuresh Kore, share insights not just into the operations and financial challenges faced, but also the human relationships, resilience, humour and practical ingenuity required to survive in the world of high-stakes corporate rescue. In vivid detail, they walk the reader through the real-world negotiations, moments of despair, flashes of hope and the hard-won lessons that can guide anyone facing uncertainty—whether in business or in life. The book is an essential read for entrepreneurs, professionals and dreamers alike: a story where endurance and adaptability win against all odds.'

**—Harit Nagpal, MD & CEO, Tata Play Ltd**

'*Rollercoaster of Hope* is a clear, ground-level story of how two co-leaders kept a theme park alive when almost everything went wrong. The bank labelled the company a bad loan. Court cases piled up. COVID shut the gates. Lenders turned hostile. It should have failed. They used one rule, 1% Hope—protect the last 1% that still works—and grow it. Not optimism, daily actions. One banker who still takes the call. One hearing that moves forward. One ride kept ready. Payroll met. Vendors paid. Numbers clean. Repeat. The leaders had different styles but one commitment. Argue in private, align in public. Block opportunists. Face banks with facts. Keep the team steady and the asset ready. Small wins add up. Time opens. Options return. This book shows how to stay the course and turn the last 1% into tomorrow.'

**—Ajay Kelkar, Leadership Coach for CXOs & Founders, TEDx Speaker, Former HDFC & Shopper's Stop CXO**

'A remarkable story of Imagicaa's comeback from the brink of financial collapse to an inspiring revival. Guided by the vision of Dhimant Bakshi and Mayuresh Kore, it reveals how resilience, determination and belief can transform even the most impossible odds. A testament to how the faintest spark of hope can fuel extraordinary change.'

**—Rakesh Biyani, Retailer**

'Dhimant and Mayuresh's story could rival any Bollywood blockbuster—packed with twists, turns, heroes and a rotating cast of villains. But beneath the drama lies a deeper story: one that highlights the power of resilient, purposeful leadership and its capacity to navigate adversity and crisis—battles that Imagicaa faced in abundance.'

**—Prof. Paddy Padmanabhan, Unilever Chaired Professor of Marketing, INSEAD**

'In the darkest hours, even a flicker of hope can steady an organisation. The Bhagavad Gita reminds us—'*Karmanye vadhikaraste ma phaleshu kadachana*'—our duty lies in action, not in outcomes, so focus on right action and keep moving. The leaders in Imagicaa have clearly lived this truth in real life, turning adversity into strength, and deployed humour to build a real muscle of tenacity. Lovely read! Recommend it to anyone wanting to learn what tenacity and resilience in a VUCA world really mean!

**—Shivam Puri, Managing Director and CEO, Cipla Health Ltd**

'This is a great story on how one should rise to the occasion when confronted with an impossible mission. Partnering with others and the conviction of stakeholders brings out the best and now at the cusp of a leapfrog. A classic!'

**—Sanjay Dutt, MD & CEO, Tata Realty & Infrastructure Limited**

'An exciting, transformational journey of Imagicaa from the brink of collapse to a remarkable turnaround. It's an unfiltered, straight from the gut story of a company seldom spoken about. With camaraderie rooted in grit and belief, the book has interesting lessons packed with wit and humour. Watch out, *Sholay*!'

**—Rajan Amba, MD & CEO, JLR India**

'This book will teach you why hope should be part of the balance sheet. This is not just the story of courage, optimism and leadership but it is the masterpiece of "turnaround by restructuring beliefs"!'

**—Prasad Chavare, Managing Director and CEO, Foseco India Limited**

'This is an extraordinary story of resilience and influence. It has the power to inspire millions. It also offers profound insights into the practical realities of running a business. The pictures bring the journey to life even more vividly. This is a truly remarkable contribution to the world. I wish all the best to the book and the authors.'

**—Harjeet Khanduja, Senior Vice President, HR, Reliance Jio**

'*Rollercoaster of Hope* is a testament to the grit and camaraderie of Dhimant, Mayuresh and colleagues as they faced one of the most tumultuous journeys in corporate history. It is a playbook for perseverance, leadership and the power of collective wisdom. The narrative captures the essence of resilience, the importance of transparent communication, and the ability to find solutions even in the darkest times. All of us face a fight-or-flee situation in our work careers, and this is a lesson on fight.

For anyone looking to understand the dynamics of leadership under pressure, the art of navigating complex deals or simply seeking inspiration to keep moving forward despite setbacks, this book is a must-read.

This journey is a reminder that hope, coupled with action, can lead to extraordinary outcomes.'

**—Kumar Rajagopalan, CEO, Retailers Association of India**

'While many readers would feel the intensity and audacity of the challenges, I am honoured to have lived some chapters with these two amazing human beings. A must-read to draw inspiration and use their ideas to help entrepreneurs overcome what each successful business and professional faces!'

**—Vishal Vithal Kamat, Executive Director, Kamat Hotels; Former Chairman, Confederation of Indian Industries (CII), Maharashtra**

'The ability to rebound, rebuild, and believe when belief itself feels scarce, that is what defines greatness. But rare is the leader who pauses and says: We have a beautiful future in our hands. These moments are far more than business decisions; they are acts of courage, responsibility and vision which inspire generations of investors and entrepreneurs to dream bigger, persevere longer and carry hope into the unknown. This book is not just a chronicle of events, it is a testament to resilience, to hope and to the kind of leadership that refuses to give up. I hope this book inspires young leaders, many of whom might have short attention spans and dreams of becoming billionaires in a rising India at a very young age.'

**—Rohit Jain, President Asia, Lionsgate Play**

'*Rollercoaster of Hope* is not just a story of Imagicaa's turnaround, it is a testament to how perseverance, resilience and decisive leadership can create value against all odds. This book doesn't just capture a corporate recovery; it narrates the journey of uncertainty and setbacks, and the quiet determination of Dhimant, Mayuresh and the entire Imagicaa team that kept them moving forward despite all the challenges life threw at them. This journey demonstrates that even in the most testing times, clarity of purpose anchored in strategy and execution can unlock opportunities and deliver extraordinary outcomes. It reaffirms a timeless truth—'within every adversity lies the seed of opportunity'.

**—Amit Gainda, MD & CEO, Avanse Financial Services**

'A book that brings to fore the true spirit of never-say-die! Truly lives through the core foundation of the Gita of not focusing on outcomes but just keep walking. A story of how one can make a meaningful and purposeful situation out of a desperate one. A very light narration of a serious subject with loads of learning—on human psychology, finance and running business with risk management. For those who take people on a ride, being taken for a ride at some situations and the learnings that came out of it, few would openly share this. Loved every bit of the book.'

**—Rajee Bhattacharyya, Co-Founder, Percipere**

'A feel-good, motivational ride that keeps you hooked from beginning till end. A never-give-up tale of leadership grit, emotional intelligence, resilience, teamwork ... and the fairytale ending of snatching victory from the jaws of defeat against all odds. What a ride!'

**—Shashank Jha, CEO & Director, Artson Ltd, a Tata Enterprise**

'I have been a partner and an observer to quite a few of Dhimant's days of labour from the early days leading up to his current assignment. *Rollercoaster of Hope* makes a great read of Dhimant's memoirs. It literally takes you through the ups and downs the team faced in turning the ship around and is a sincere account of the journey. It's well-written, lucid and engaging.'

**—Sanjay Vakharia, Co-Founder and CEO, Spykar Lifestyles Pvt. Ltd**

'A powerful story of grit and resilience, this book shows how adversity shapes true leadership. Every struggle becomes a teacher, every challenge a path to growth. It is a timeless lesson in motivation, focus, and transformation.'

**—Gautam Khanna, CEO, P D Hinduja Hospital & MRC, Mumbai**

'Any enterprise building is like a long-term relationship—a product of a lot of love, commitment, integrity and collaboration for a common end. The way Mr Dhimant Bakshi and Mr Mayuresh Kore have worked through the maze of processes to rejuvenate the Imagicaa experience as narrated in this book is reflective of these principles laced with empathy for all those individuals and small enterprises having dependencies on them. Sure to be inspiring reading, and may be each reader can pocket some lessons for themselves along the ride despite slides through crests and troughs!'

**—Roop Rashi, CEO, KVIC, Government of India**

'I have been closely associated with the Imagicaa theme park since inception, having done their first equity raise from ICICI Venture in 2013, and it's great to see the business flourishing now. Dhimant and Mayuresh have always shown a don't-give-up attitude in anything they do, and this book is a practical masterclass on how to navigate financial stress and bring the business back. A valuable learning in today's ever-changing business world.'

**—Vishal Mahajan, Director, *Times of India***

'This book is a love letter to audacity and endurance. If dreams are oxygen, grit is the lung. Here's to the audacity that birthed the new Imagicaa, and to the grit that kept her heartbeat steady when silence was the loudest sound. Watching Dhimant and Mayuresh stand between despair and hope taught me that leadership is not titles—it's stamina, humility and the courage to ask again. It's the art of converting scars into stripes!'

**—Vineet Majgaonkar, Chairman, Armstrong Dematic**

'Exciting journey of Imagicaa well driven by Dhimant, Mayuresh and team, which turned adversity in opportunity with trusting their intuition and top-notch execution at every stage. To navigate through tough times including that of COVID-19 and transforming into a complete business turnaround of a highly seasonal and complex format is truly commendable.'

**—Karan Taurani, Executive Vice President, Elara Capital**

'Circa 2010, DEI joined Imagicaa when the park was still just a vision on a hillside. From day one, we shared in the dream of creating India's first truly world-class theme park destination. When the gates opened in 2013, Imagicaa set a new benchmark for entertainment in the country, drawing families from Mumbai, Pune and far beyond. Over the past decade, while capturing millions of guest memories, we've also witnessed the park's own rollercoaster ride—its spectacular highs, daunting lows and inspiring resurgence. Through every turn, our collaboration with Dhimant and the Imagicaa team has been anchored in innovation, resilience and the shared goal of enriching every guest experience. And just like the rides it's famous for, Imagicaa has proven that with strong foundations and a determined spirit, every dip is followed by a greater rise.'

**—Swetha Prabhakaran, President, Global Business Development and Marketing, DEI (Digiphoto Entertainment Imaging)**

# Rollercoaster of Hope

*The Turnaround Story of Imagicaa*

Dhimant Bakshi
& Mayuresh Kore

WESTLAND
**BUSINESS**

WESTLAND
**BUSINESS**

Published by Westland Business, an imprint of Westland Books, a division of Nasadiya Technologies Private Limited, in 2025

No. 269/2B, First Floor, 'Irai Arul', Vimalraj Street, Nethaji Nagar, Alapakkam Main Road, Maduravoyal, Chennai 600095



ISBN: 9789371975490

10 9 8 7 6 5 4 3 2 1



Typeset by Mukul

Printed at Parksons Graphics Pvt. Ltd

*To the millions of happy guests at Imagicaa for their unwavering trust in us.*

*There's no better magic than their smiles, which sparked our hope and belief through this arduous journey.*

# Contents

# Foreword

Our journey with Dhimant and Mayuresh began in 2019, when Imagicaa was facing its toughest years. The company stood on the brink of bankruptcy, yet what stood out was their commitment and resilience. Against all odds, they upheld guest standards, maintained assets, motivated teams and managed lenders with rare grit and calm.

COVID-19 only deepened the crisis, but instead of retreating, their resolve grew stronger. From reopening parks during each unlock phase, to chasing tax refunds, to keeping the box office alive with creative promotions, their determination never faltered.

What we saw was not just management, but intrapreneurship at its best. They went far beyond defined roles, pulling the company back from the brink. Both authors regularly engaged with our partners, gaining a deep understanding of the operating parameters. Their insights and involvement were instrumental in shaping the transaction in its entirety, creating a favourable structure and a true win-win for all stakeholders.

Through it all, they never lost their humour, quick thinking and optimism. Their resilience and refusal to give up laid the foundation for Imagicaa's journey—from 'survive' to 'revive' and ultimately to 'thrive'.

This book is not just about hardships. It is a playbook of perseverance, immense optimism and resilience, and a testament to how leadership is tested not in easy times but in the storms. Dhimant and Mayuresh stood firm in that storm, and this is their story.

**Jai Malpani**
Managing Director, Imagicaaworld Entertainment Limited

# In Gratitude

We are grateful to our promoters, the Malpani family and the Shetty family, for their faith and support in this entire journey. At various junctures, they have entrusted us with pivotal assignments, and we hope that we were able to live up to the expectations.

Sincere thanks to Manmohan Sir, Pooja and Aarti Shetty for their grand vision, unlimited zeal, pioneering efforts to imagine and build a project of such scale and class in record time, with top-notch rides and equipment blended with Indian stories and sensibilities and an amazing storytelling approach. It transformed the lives of many and changed the way Indians got entertained, democratising entertainment in its true sense.

Special mention of Jai Malpani, the young scion of the Malpani family who, with his strong business acumen, unlimited patience, ability to listen, observe and absorb, kept the resolution process on with grace and kind demeanour. Jai, whom we saw as a young man of just twenty-four then, under the able guidance of Rajesh Malpani, Manish Malpani and the family board members, held on to the threads that ultimately led to a landmark transaction in the Indian debt resolution sphere, a takeover which tried to be as fair to the existing stakeholders as possible. For most of us, it felt like a merger.

We are truly indebted to have been surrounded by highly committed and capable colleagues who stuck through this journey as a strong, united team.

Our independent directors stood their ground and guided us like a lighthouse through these critical junctures. They were available on short notice and would listen to the situation and guide us most ably.

Further, it is truly commendable that the Malpani Group have continued with existing leadership teams and independent directors post their takeover. This resulted in a strong sense of continuity and stability across the organisation.

Special mention to our better halves, Toral Bakshi and Roshani Kore, for always being there as pillars of strength through the rollercoaster and standing by our side, irrespective of the situation. They are our true sources of strength and dedication.

Our children, Dhyey and Tanay Bakshi, Devayani and Amodini Kore, with their happiness and enthusiasm, lightened the mood however our (usually long) day would have been. Many a times, with their innocent questions based upon what they heard from their friends, also kept us abreast of public opinions ☺!

To our parents, who imparted values that forged a strong foundation. With a clear belief system, they taught us to be good and do good with courage and conviction. To our in-laws, for their blessings and good wishes, which helped us tide over difficult times and stay steady through this journey.

To our brothers, co-brothers, in-laws and extended families for being the guiding light for us, validating our thoughts and always being supportive and standing by us through thick and thin.

To our mentors, who inspired and moulded us as people, great colleagues and friends who at various junctures in our careers (and their careers too!) stood by us as well as became sounding boards and, with the right nudges, helped us connect the dots and make sense of situations.

As a token of our gratitude for this book seeing the light of day in the literary world, all royalties from this book shall be donated to the Antarang Foundation, TRRAIN and the under privileged in the vicinity of our parks.

Many people helped us, some even without having met us. It is simply unbelievable who can play the role of a messiah in your journey and, even before one realises their contribution, they are long gone from the situation. Thank you to those who may not have been mentioned in this book.

Further, sincere apologies to those whose sentiments may have been inadvertently hurt by our words or actions while we were on our task—we hope you can forgive and forget!

# Authors' Note

THE ETHOS AND PURPOSE BEHIND WRITING THIS BOOK IS TO light the way in challenging journeys with hope and belief, whatever the odds may be. We hope someone somewhere can get little nuggets or inspirations to address their challenging situations with collective wisdom, camaraderie and with a never-say-never spirit, even in the worst of times.

We had to set aside our biases and preferences, approaching the situation with an open mind, willingness to collaborate and the desire for a win-win outcome for all stakeholders.

We walked together, even as the two of us are very different personalities. Somewhere along the way, we understood that we needed to complement one another in the best possible manner and how to do it. This partnership made a strong structure, like a textile warp and weft running perpendicular to each other, and allowed us to look at various situations, opportunities and problems with a very unique and out-of-the-box approach.

While this is a journey that describes how we dodged a bankruptcy situation, the underlying approach is what will help anyone in any sphere. With that belief, we have shared some of the many events that we experienced. In fact, it is heart-warming that a few corporate leaders have already reached out to us to share our experiences and learnings with their leadership teams. We were enthused to see how their teams appreciated the stories and lessons from our experience.

It is eventually a 'leap of faith' that gets you beyond the normal. This book is dedicated to all the wonderful people out there doing their best in their own walks of life and requiring that nudge to cross over to the other side.

Here's a real story of a turnaround for you. Hope you enjoy reading it and find some value in it.

# Introduction

In June 2018, Imagicaa, India's biggest theme park, turned into a non-performing asset (NPA) as its ninety-day window of paying interest on loans worth over ₹1,020 crore closed. This led to the company being classified as a defaulter, as the last extended date of paying instalment on loans had passed.

Imagicaa. India's first integrated entertainment destination. The park was founded by Manmohan Shetty. At the time, this was the largest private investment in an amusement park. The property comprised an international standard theme park, water park and a five-star deluxe hotel strategically located between Mumbai and Pune at Khopoli. The park housed some of the best-in-class rides and equipment, thematic shows and experiences. It had set out to bring an experience comparable to Disney and Universal to our backyard, and at one-fourth the price.

Destiny, however, had other plans. The NPA announcement was only the first in a series of events to follow.

Most creditors typically spend a year discussing possible resolutions with a company, but within a month of turning NPA, Imagicaa was forced to start fighting for survival in the National Company Law Tribunal (NCLT) courts. Problems were soon getting fast forwarded, with no solution in sight.

To add to our woes, within two years of this, COVID-19's malevolent shadow fell on the world and enforced a complete shutdown of most businesses. Imagicaa had to shut its doors to customers as the world was engulfed in a never-before-seen pandemic. The company's share price hit an all-time low of ₹3.3, signalling the markets' dim perception of its future. Imagicaa was an outdoor recreational entertainment park, all about the great experiences with friends and family. With the mandatory social distancing, there was going to be no near-term respite for the company.

These were dark years, full of strife and numerous battles; years when many questioned Imagicaa's survival and why we had still not quit. According to most experts, Imagicaa was not supposed to survive those lean years, when even the operational income that kept the business machinery moving was lost due to COVID-19 regulations and Imagicaa's massive rollercoasters fell silent.

Then in 2023 our world revolved again …

Imagicaa's market capitalisation stood at a whopping ₹4,000 crore! This implied that almost the entire principal from the ten lender banks that had been outstanding till it turned NPA had been recovered, as they had been issued equity of ₹75 crore as part of the settlement at a price of ₹15.3, while the price reached ₹75+ in 2023.

This time we were asked a different set of questions:

- How on the earth did you guys manage this turnaround despite all contrary market predictions?

- What kept Imagicaa going?
- How could you maintain the assets and reopen on unlock notices so quickly?
- And more importantly, what can other such beleaguered companies learn from this?

In fact, this astounding value was not unanticipated.

Imagicaa was a dream project with an audacious ambition to create a truly world-class theme park in India. The intention was to create a park with homegrown stories well blended with global standard attractions, rides, slides and equipment that were thoroughly researched. The benchmark was the best attractions in global parks. With an intent to revolutionise and democratise entertainment in India, no stone was left unturned to make it truly world class. The approach was to achieve scale a few notches below Disney or Universal, rather than seeking to create something a few notches above the other available options in India. Mr Shetty often referred to this approach as 'minus being greater than plus' ( – > + ). The park was designed to serve over three million visitors a year, which was truly large by any imagination with expectations of higher ARPUs (average revenue per user). The belief was that even in seasons like the monsoon, we would see decent footfalls from a section of people who visit Lonavala, a popular hill station and tourist destination near Mumbai, as Imagicaa was just 25 km away.

The project was a combination of a global-standard theme park, high-quality water park with gold-standard water filtration that met world-class hygiene. In addition, a five-star deluxe hotel on the property made it an integrated entertainment project designed to be a national tourism destination.

Of course, this was based on significant impetus in form of a fast-growing younger populace as a favourable demographical trend coupled with upcoming infrastructure such as a new airport in Navi Mumbai, improved road connectivity, the Trans Harbour Link, extended railway lines and so on, all of which were envisaged in the feasibility stage.

Interestingly, during all the conversations with potential investors, we usually projected a conservative EBITDA of ₹80 crore. We knew that our business fundamentals were strong. The problem lay in the huge loan overhang. Of course, most investors smirked or even laughed out loud when we showed our projected value. They thought we were spinning piped dreams out of sheer desperation to rope in an investor. Achieving an EBITDA of ₹100 crore in 2023, after Imagicaa was successfully acquired by the Sangamner-based Malpani Group as strategic promoters in June 2022, validated the strong promoter acumen and our belief in Imagicaa's potential. This increase in company valuation also proved to be a windfall for the banks who had earlier told us that our shares (which were part of the payment in the final settlement) were just 'valueless paper'. Thanks to those shares, the banks now received a significantly higher recovery than was agreed and expected!

What is the story behind this revival from the brink? How did two professionals—Dhimant Bakshi and Mayuresh Kore, both with divergent approaches in life—align their ways to achieve the larger goals and navigate out of so many tricky situations?

## Twists and Turns

When Dhimant took on the mantle as the joint CEO of Imagicaa in 2017, he knew the business involved rollercoasters, but he never anticipated that this journey would shunt us into a real-life rollercoaster ride, full of blinding twists and heart-pumping turns and falls.

Nothing really prepares you for running a company that has been qualified as an NPA by lender banks and is battling for survival in the National Company Law Tribunal (NCLT) courts. He was especially at a loss because he comes from a retail background—what was referred to as a *dukaandaar background*—and had never had to deal with corporate finance, leave aside a complex case of a financial crisis. In a career spanning thirty-odd years, he had worked in retail positions across companies like Shoppers' Stop, Future Group, Reliance Retail and Globus before joining Imagicaa as a retail business head in 2012. A format like Imagicaa Retail did not exist in India at the time. It had to be created, and the idea of working on a completely blank slate and meeting new challenges excited him. Personally, the timing couldn't have been better. Joining Imagicaa was a big leap of faith, and I think such decisions are taken from the heart. You can't think through them.

He loved challenges, and somehow, since the beginning of his career, he had faced constant change and fluidity, so it had almost become second nature to him. His friends often joked that a steady state wasn't meant for him!

When he joined, it was clear that the park (the rides and the hotel) would generate all the revenue, while the retail department was to be a fringe department. No one expected much out of retail, and that was a challenge he was willing to accept. In hindsight, this situation was great. In the first year itself, the retail vertical started generating almost 8% of the total revenue despite miniscule resources. But managing a company that was going through NCLT courts and NPA proceedings led him into unknown territory, with a wide variety of investors—from elite professionals to phonies and professional conmen!

No one warns you about this. Neither management schools nor courses talk about how to scout for genuine investors in this all-consuming quicksand that abounds with scamsters, frauds and ego-centric middlemen. No 'communication for dummies' on how to speak, build and maintain trust in a way that ensures genuine investors don't lose interest due to the chaos caused by the phony or unsuitable investors. Furthermore, how to create a win-win situation for all stakeholders and keep the apple cart moving.

This tricky marshland is not visible at first. It lies hidden behind the obvious glare of start-ups, self-proclaimed experts and successful companies. As we walked through this unfamiliar territory, we realised it hides many false prophets and their bugle blowers. However, it also revealed amazing teammates, true friends and hidden gems who surprised us with guest appearances and strengthened us at crucial junctures.

Mayuresh had also been integral part of Imagicaa's fund raising process as well as the project and had risen to become its CFO in October 2016. His knowledge of banks, strong grasp of the situation and an excellent relationship with almost everyone helped the company avoid many pitfalls that we would have unknowingly walked into.

At Imagicaa we both ran into each other at a very awkward time, and ended up becoming 2 a.m. friends, confidants and partners-in-adventures as we navigated our way through this hair-raising journey.

There were so many aspects to manage; and we can truthfully say that we managed what we could, when we could. Yet when we look back, there are certain things that we know we learnt that can help other business leaders and owners navigate these trying times and answers questions like:

- What happens when you go to the NCLT court?
- How do you manage NCLT matters, bankers, valuation, promoters and stakeholders?
- How do you build resilience and keep your team aligned through this testing time?

- How do you continue to maintain guest experience standards of a superlative nature?

## The Two Amigos or *Do Bechare*

As we battled through those years, the two of us were often laughingly referred to by our senior colleague with his unmatchable wit as '*Do bechare, bina sahare*' and eventually by many people we met. As we were buffeted from one crisis to another, it didn't seem like too far-fetched a description.

In fact, we attended many morbid meetings, during which our interlocutors tried to hammer in the idea that Imagicaa was doomed. Some of our industry peers also spread faulty rumours about our company that would give us a shaky start in these meetings. We often think that these meetings should have left us feeling hopeless, but both of us were driven by our common goal of reviving Imagicaa. We wanted to repay all our loans because we truly believed in Imagicaa's asset quality, vision and business proposition and the happiness that it brought to millions of guests. So after every such meeting, as we would walk away and sombrely discuss what everyone had said, somewhere a funny one-liner or a high-five moment would arise, making us laugh out loud at our situation and at life in oddest of hours. That was enough to move on to another day. You could call us foolhardy with an untimely sense of humour, or you could call us the two crazy amigos who always found a laugh or a chuckle to close a disastrous day. Looking back, it kept us moving forward day after day.

This is a true story of our lives over five years. Both of us had some adventures, misadventures and heart-pounding situations that we have tried to capture in this book. We hope that you will enjoy it while you read and laugh through this journey. We believe that our learnings can be useful in your journey too.

At times, you may need time and patience to figure out who is narrating the story, but know that is exactly how we lived it. Our days and adventures were intertwined, and so is our story. If you can't at times figure out who is the narrator, that's exactly how it was possibly destined to be!

*Amigo Mantra #1:* Udte teer se bachna zaroori hai, aur sab friends zaroori hai. *To survive you need good friends as shields and the wisdom to stay away from flying arrows above and landmines below!*

*Amigo Mantra #2:* Sir salamat to pagdi hazaar. *Let's see what tomorrow brings! Caps are in plenty if you have your head intact! Survive today and see what tomorrow brings.*

# 1

# Of Thick Skins and Messy Claims

*'Amarnath, by refreshing your computer screen, we will not get funds. Go home now, it's midnight!'*

On 26 June 2018, Imagicaa exceeded the ninety-day period in paying its interest of ₹120 crore on its loan of over ₹1,000 crore. As per banking norms, if a company's interest payment is delayed over ninety days, its classification drops further from SMA 2 (i.e. principal or interest payment overdue between 61–90 days) and it becomes a non-performing asset (NPA). Until then, our finance team had always managed to pay the interest in the nick of time by managing somehow through borrowings or some other means. However, the principal repayment was structured to be of a ballooning type, meaning that instalments were smaller in the early stages and would increase later, which allowed the business to stabilise. Some of us knew that after two or three years, the monthly debt burden would undoubtedly increase—we were headed for a debt trap.

| Year | Loan Amount | Interest Payment | EBITDA | Deficit (Gap) |
|---|---|---|---|---|
| 2013–17 | ₹1,000 crore | ₹120 crore | ₹53 crore | ₹60–70 crore |
| 2015 (Public Issue) | ₹330 crore (raised) | | | Temporary liquidity boost, gap still existing |
| 2016–17 (IL&FS Offer) | ₹1,000 crore Debt + ₹190 crore acquisition | ₹120 crore | | Gap continues |
| 2018 (NPA) | N/A | ₹120 crore | ₹53 crore | N/A |

Imagicaa never earned more than ₹53 crore EBIDTA net. Never. So, there was a deficit of upwards of ₹60 crore each year in the money going towards the interest payment ever since we started. Yet, because it was a good project with immense potential, investors saw its worth and we kept on finding ways to service the loan.

In 2015, we had come out with a public issue that raised ₹330 crore. Our debt reduced for a brief period, and we got liquidity and a reputational boost.

In 2016, IL&FS had approached us with an offer, and after a few months of data crunching and scenario building, they said they would give us ₹1000 crore as debt and a further ₹190 crore to acquire another theme park in Delhi. The draft proposal was too good to be true and somehow, whenever we visited their head office, we felt something was not right. The financial circles also buzzed with whispers of financial instability. Finally, we didn't go ahead with the deal, which turned out to be a good thing, because in 2017 the major issues at IL&FS came to light. This large institution went bust, shaking the overall financial system of the country and had a ripple effect, especially on *marginal* borrowers. We were back to facing a shortfall every year.

Finally, with virtually no choice to bridge the financial gap in 2016, we borrowed money by pledging the shares of Mr Shetty, the promoter of Imagicaa, to Edelweiss. This way we kept the machine moving ... *gaadi chal rahi thi.*

Amarnath, one of the employees from our finance department, had seen how the finance head always found a way through and he was still hoping for a miracle on that fateful day in June 2018 when we were turning NPA. He kept on tapping the Refresh (F5) key of the computer in the vain hope that the funds to pay our interest (₹10 crore) would magically appear and the ship of Imagicaa would continue sailing for one more month without sinking. Even now, he was hoping some inflow from somewhere—a promoter, investor or some form of bridge funding, like before.

We knew this wouldn't happen. Not this time.

As that disastrous day was unfolding, Dhimant could not help but think about the repercussions of becoming an NPA on day-to-day operations. We had all heard of companies that turned NPA, but what did it mean in reality? What were the implications for the company, the promoters, employees, board members and key management personnel? How would we hold the team together, find good investors, manage payment to suppliers and stay afloat till we found a lasting solution? Since the Prudential Framework and the bankruptcy code was still evolving, there were a lot of ambiguities back then.

### Walking into the Ring

It was supposed to be a small corporate party in September 2017. The party had started with a mini town hall of forty-odd senior and mid-level executives when Kapil Bagla, then CEO of Imagicaa, took the mic and announced that he was moving on. The new CEO position would now be shared by Col. Ashutosh Kale and Dhimant Bakshi! Everyone in the room was startled and began exchanging glances.

Mayuresh has been a part of Imagicaa since its inception, so people started looking at him as if he would definitely know what was happening. He had a difficult time trying to tell them that this was news for him too.

If Mayuresh was surprised, Dhimant froze hearing this; and friends will tell you that this miraculous event is very rare, where you are announced as Jt CEO without any prior notice or inkling of a changeover.

In July 2017, two months before we took charge, Imagicaa got a D rating by credit rating agencies (D here meant 'default category'). Imagicaa's finances were being discussed fairly openly in business circles. Yet, at this unexpected appointment to the role, he felt truly overwhelmed—a mix of exuberance and cynicism.

The Joint CEO role meant that Col. Kale, his senior counterpart, would run overall park operations and safety in Khopoli (where the park was located, 90 km from Greater Mumbai), while Dhimant would manage business functions with P&L ownership and brand custodianship directly, and drive debt resolution alongside Mayuresh as CFO. It seemed a good demarcation of roles, but there were enough naysayers who predicted a fallout of the two due to the arrangement. Even before the D rating, we knew that Imagicaa needed strong corporate finance corrections.

Most experts and people didn't view the CEO role positively. They were right in their own way, yet this was a responsibility placed on us and we wanted to execute it to the best of our abilities. We have always been grateful to the Shetty family for their trust in us. Dhimant in particular had worked with both Pooja and Aarti, Mr Shetty's daughters. Pooja especially had an ever-enthusiastic and astute approach to brand building, marketing, F&B and retail. For Dhimant, it came as a blessing in disguise to get an opportunity of this magnitude with absolutely no corporate finance background, considering the nature of the problem at hand. Mayuresh had worked a lot with the Shetty family, as he had already been part of the earlier venture too.

Despite Dhimant's non-finance background, it did not take long for him to understand the dismal status of our finances. The sombre mood of the D rating was reflected in the first board meeting that he attended after embracing this new role, when an independent director took him aside and advised in a grandfatherly tone, 'This is a sinking ship, but I am not a rat. However, frankly I don't see much hope of survival.' It wasn't the rosiest of predictions, and a jarring induction to the hallowed board meetings that usually happened once a quarter but coloured the entire year. While his intention was very noble and he advised Dhimant to fasten the seatbelt, the timing was unbelievable.

On the other hand, Mayuresh was fully aware of the issues surrounding the finances. Dhimant often said that Mayuresh was the 'archives section' of Imagicaa, full of information.

In fact, more than a year earlier in March 2017, the two of us had had a full-blown argument about a media for equity deal with the Times Group that he wanted to be rolled out immediately. Incidentally, this was Mayuresh's first professional interaction with him. This face-off was because Dhimant thought that, despite following up a few times, there had been limited action from his end on this deal. The deal would have reduced our cash outflow, and getting right mediums of advertising to push the brand visibility and campaigns was the idea.

Mayuresh clearly seemed to have different priorities or was letting the proposal lose steam is what Dhimant thought. He remembers saying this and the altercation that followed. This was very unlike him, but in the heat of the moment, Dhimant exclaimed, 'It's not done to have an indifferent or irresponsible approach to the company requirement!' Later, only when he entered the scene, he understood the gravity of the situation Mayuresh was facing. But he didn't offer any explanation for his attitude, neither did he share what the issue was. Somehow, it was always handled as a confidential matter and not shared clearly even with the remaining leadership team. Perhaps this attitude was counterproductive, as informing senior people would have allowed each one to participate and contribute to the solutions in their own space.

The finance team was constantly trying to manage the interest payments and keep the ship afloat, and we never really told anyone about what deadlines we were facing.

On 31 March 2017, we had to desperately get a loan disbursement from our banker. Mayuresh was sitting at the branch the whole day, almost like a bank employee, waiting to get that money out, because if the process was delayed to the next day, then things might change. Bank closure day is on

1 April, and as the bankers reviewed the accounts, some other issue might suddenly come up. We had to get that loan that day. Yet no one from any other department would understand what we were struggling with.

Interestingly, before Dhimant's very first meeting with the board of directors, Mayuresh had briefed him to answer only when it was absolutely necessary, and when a question was directed at him specifically, to answer in monosyllables. Mayuresh was the one who usually updated the board about the business and led the proceedings knowing what would sail through and what could cause a furore. However, at a critical juncture, without warning, he instinctively directed Dhimant to conduct the proceedings. It was like sending a young featherweight boxer without the essential mouthguard to face the likes of Muhammad Ali in the corporate world! However, he handled it with ease. He maintained his poise, and somewhere he realised that this situation would need a calm attitude. The bewildered look he had at the time is unforgettable.

Something had to give financially, and it finally did. We had started speaking to experts and were told that becoming an NPA didn't mean that the company would get immediately shut down. There are many stages in an NPA situation. 'Getting classified as an NPA is not the end, but don't forget to wear guards while you prepare for the new innings,' they added with a wicked smile.

We were told that the process would begin with the Imagicaa account getting transferred to the stressed asset vertical of the lender banks and would be dealt with differently. The team that often handles such cases is the 'Recovery Department', and its purpose is to maximise recovery from the defaulters.

Yes. Stress was a much-used word during that time. Financial stress, stressed vertical, company in stress, stressed people. No wonder it led to stress all around.

'Develop a thick skin and wear a wooden smile,' our investor relations advisor from SGA, Samir Shah, told us crisply. Samir was a wise man, and we had gone to him to seek advice on how to steer the ship, considering that he had handled a massive amount of debt as a professional CFO.

We were warned to get ready for some really harsh treatment. Some borrowers turn into wilful defaulters, and this has created an air of negativity towards all defaulters, leading to them receiving rough treatment. Recovery teams have started handling all cases with a common method and a heavily coloured lens. We understood their predicament and never really blamed them or expected any special treatment. It was a clear case of inability to differentiate wheat from the chaff. Furthermore, the stressed asset verticals, which handle such accounts, have no detailed background of what has transpired and why for specific cases. Thus, the forensic assessment begins with a check for any financial shenanigans or the misappropriation of funds.

Everyone we met gave us a set of warnings:

> 'Lenders will start doubting your words and ask your promoters to bridge the gap.'
>
> 'People start will thinking that company funds have been diverted elsewhere, depriving the rightful lenders. You've had it if you get wrongly tagged as a "wilful defaulter".'
>
> 'Personal guarantees, corporate guarantees and valuation *pe hi gaadi chalegi, bhaiya*.'

## Of Deal Makers and Breakers

The management had known that time was running out and we had already started looking to sell non-core assets to investors or buyers. We had classified the park itself as a core asset, whereas undeveloped land and the hotel that were a part of the property were categorised as non-core assets. Selling these would help us reduce the debt burden and adopt debt restructuring schemes like S4A or 5/25 from the Prudential Framework.

In fact, in November 2017, a well-respected billionaire investor with a solid reputation had been interested in our hotel property with 287 rooms, which was partly commissioned with 116 rooms in the first phase and had shown good traction in a short span of time. The pending 171 rooms were expected to be commissioned in the next few months.

We allowed ourselves to hope. Maybe, as we started on this new role in Imagicaa, this opportunity could be Phase 2 for both of us. Right after Dhimant became the CEO, the term sheet for the sale of the hotel was being signed by our erstwhile CEO. It seemed like a landmark moment, and we were joyous, expecting to make quicker progress now. This could have paved a pathway to a faster restructuring with the lenders. Little did we know that the runway we thought was in front of us had potholes!

Through this deal, the company planned to sell the hotel along with some adjacent land. The investor planned to infuse more money into the hotel and build more banqueting facilities, and also build a budget hotel in the additional land. The deal also meant that Mr Shetty would still be in the driver's seat of the company, and lenders would be repaid to the quantum of the hotel sale proceeds. This would reduce the outstanding debt by almost 20%. Of course, we were delighted; yet, when the time for the signing came, basic due diligence led to the discovery of a major complication.

You see, before investing in large properties, buyers usually put an ad in the papers informing the public of their intention. This is to check if there are any other claimants to the land, as opposed to the seller being the sole rightful owner of the property.

Usually, this is just a formality, but in our case, a claimant turned up for a small parcel of the land. He knew the significance of his parcel of land and played his cards to service his greed and continued to litigate against us.

This problem had its roots to the time when Imagicaa was taking shape. In 2009, Mr Shetty spent a lot of time hunting for suitable land parcels to build his dream park. Many boxes had to be ticked: it had to be around 300 acres, ideally located, not too expensive and free of litigation. A single landowner with a large land bank was next to impossible to find. At the time of buying the land, our legal team vetted the title deeds sent by the land aggregators because there were multiple tracts of land (more than a hundred land parcels), and you had to rely upon the brokers and aggregators.

Since 2011, there had been an ongoing case by one person against the land aggregator for some tracts of land. The claimant turned out to be highly obdurate and stubborn. When the hotel sale ad came out in the papers, he saw an opportunity to raise the stakes and began sending notices, ultimately triggering a petition opposing the sale of the hotel. Despite being the legitimate land owners, we were pulled into a messy legal battle. Land litigation is usually a long-drawn-out affair in India and potential buyers understandably want to deal with a clear and marketable title.

Our investor now wanted an exit. But it was not that easy. Much before this claimant turned up, when everything seemed to be moving in the right direction, our investor had given Imagicaa a token advance of ₹15 crore in good faith and based on the merit of the business. He had not demanded any comfort or guarantee for that money. It was a gentleman's promise. Now, when the litigant raked up the issue, everything we did started being viewed through a lens of suspicion by the lawyers and professional consultants.

During some of these court/arbitrator hearings and all the preparatory meetings, the interactions with the lawyers increased multifold. Furthermore, because of how much we had to wait for each step forward, we had a chance to have various conversations. One such conversation was one we had with a senior counsel. He chuckled and said, 'Look, you got to pay someone in this process, either a black coat who will help you with the process and fight for you, or the litigant, who will give you an outcome—choice is yours. Since you are all sinking, you may just want to think about it.'

As the hotel sale deal eventually collapsed, the advance amount received became immediately payable, but there was no way we could pay it. Despite all our good intentions, we added another black mark against our name. Nevertheless, the investor and his team acted like thorough gentlemen and still met us respectfully because both of us were clear that the advance deposit had to be repaid. We wanted to be transparent. However, this matter had led to a big embarrassment and created a huge trust deficit. We felt the best way was to keep the communication channel open and keep the investor abreast of the current status and any ongoing developments, whatever they might be.

Cut to that fateful day in June 2018, when the ninety-day interest payment timeline expired, we sat with the members of the finance team—Arvind, Sarafat and Amarnath—in our office late in the evening. We had mentally walked out of the 'we-might-turn-into-an-NPA' door and entered the 'we-are-an-NPA' zone. We were already thinking about what new problems the next day would bring. This is when Dhimant saw Amarnath refreshing his screen again and again, and finally snapped, 'Amarnath, by refreshing your computer screen, we will not get funds. Go home now, it's midnight!'

The day was over.

*Amigo Mantra #3: Develop a thick skin, and don't forget to smile.*

*Amigo Mantra #4:* Koi maare taana, koi gaaye gaana. Chalte hi jaana, chalte hi jaana ... *The journey will be a mixed bag full of taunts, false promises or even true praise. Don't get too happy and don't get too sad, just keep moving.*

## Thought #1: The Underlying Fundamentals

Imagicaa was the vision of Manmohan Shetty, a towering figure in the Indian entertainment industry since the 1980s. His films, like *Ardh Satya* (1983) and *Gangaajal* (2003), won national awards. He also founded and developed Adlabs Films Ltd, one of India's largest media and entertainment firms and a pioneer in the film processing segment. Mr Shetty's visionary outlook led to the first IMAX dome theatre in the country and a string of multiplexes, again first of their kind.

In 2008, Mr Shetty turned towards creating a world-class theme park destination in India. Among many things, such as hair-raising rides, a haunted fort, a 4D game, thematic attractions and indigenous park characters, it was going to be India's biggest theme park destination. It was an audacious dream and a big investment of time and money. A project of this scale is not just a business idea; it requires a visionary to execute it. Mr Shetty was one of the few people who could have such an audacious dream and execute this world-class idea with a meticulous plan and fervour.

From the beginning, Imagicaa was never an easy project. It had no precedents or anything close to it in India. Again, it turned out to be a pioneering effort to meet global standards. The ambition was great, but the gap between these two was enormous, it was almost a different measure of comparison. Then came finding the right land, developing the right mix of rides and creating the entire walkthrough of the park, which took five years, while finding the finances took another two years. This audacious dream brought together a mix of doers, visionaries, planners, storytellers, illustrators, architects, engineers, financers and, of course, dreamers. Everyone on this project, no matter how prosaic or business-minded they were, had that streak of dreaming the unimaginable. That indomitable streak kept them going through the many iterations and revisions of the plan, as everyone worked to create the best mix of rides, walkways and themes that would get millions of people to come again and again.

Raising the capital for the project was a massive achievement, as no one had attempted this for an entertainment project in India before. It helped that Kapil Bagla, who was a former investment banker, was himself the CEO of the company. Along with Mayuresh and the dedicated syndication team from Centrum Capital, this gargantuan exercise was finally completed in March March 2012, a process of two-odd years. A clutch of thirteen lenders, mostly public sector banks, came together and formed a consortium for this purpose. Mr Shetty had put in a chunk of the equity, but he needed to tie up the balance equity for financial closure. That is when a relatively young yet seasoned deal maker—Vishal Mahajan, part of the investment banking team of a private bank—made his mark and got a marquee private equity fund to fill the lion's share of the balance equity gap. The remaining equity later came from a foreign investor with a team led by Rajendra Naik from Centrum Capital Market team.

During the project days, this motley crew had to work closely to achieve the objective, manage the tough timelines and overcome multiple challenges that cropped up each day. With a mix of international (Australians, Italians, Filipinos, Americans, Britishers) and domestic professionals who had never worked together, it was chaotic, as one may imagine. The key factor that kept it going was of course Mr Shetty, who inspired everyone with his hands-on approach and simple manner. We all started sharing his vision, and the project came so close to our hearts that it was no longer just another job. We all were closely involved even in activities such as naming the rides, brand creation, handling local politicos, getting past regulatory bottlenecks and so on, apart from our regular tasks.

Imagicaa as a destination was developed on the premise that it would cater to 3 million people. In fact, a feasibility study and a budget for the park was created by a reputed global consultancy firm and later, a well-known Indian agency also validated this plan. Everyone at that time believed that this number of 3 million was possible. Based on those projections, an initial budget of ₹2,200 crore was drawn up, which was later downscaled to ₹1,650 crore by Mr Shetty himself. Out of the ₹1,650 crore, the company equity component was ₹550 crore and the remaining capital was to be borrowed from thirteen lender banks.

Our business is highly driven by ongoing trends and depends a lot on inbound tourism with a steady influx over the years. It is dependent on the attention of the public, availability of time and ease of accessing the location. Further, what no one realised at that time was that the nature of our business is highly seasonal and cyclical. So if there is a blockbuster movie or an IPL match on the weekend or heavy rainfalls, then the footfalls have high chances of being divided. The monsoon will see fewer visitors in the theme park, while the water park will also get fewer visitors in winter. While there is a high capacity in the parks, there is always a limit in the number of visitors we can allow in each park to maintain the guest experience, especially on peak days. Plus, the studies also made various assumptions on infrastructural developments and tourism promotion by the government. From an infrastructure perspective, the assumptions were that the Navi Mumbai Airport would commence operations in 2014, which will improve inbound tourism, the Trans Harbour Sea Link would be ready by 2013 and Khopoli Pali Road four-laning would be done by the time we started. The latter finally happened in 2021! Also, the study anticipated that additional railway tracks would increase the frequency of local trains to Khopoli. All these initiatives would improve overall connectivity and reduce the travel time and significantly increase the addressable population. In contrast, we don't have public transport to our doorstep or even within 3 km of our location till date! All these points added up to a much lower number than the studies projected.

Our actual footfall numbers varied from 1.3 million to 1.5 million. We could possibly push harder and bridge it to 2 million, but 3 million seemed a distant dream. If we hit that number, it could potentially spoil the guest experience, unless the crowd was spread uniformly on all day or with a little standard deviation, which would defy the hospitality business pattern and was a pipe dream. Most parks in the country were nowhere close to these footfalls or revenue numbers, yet the bridge for us was too far.

The maths was simple, but the consequences stark as the years went by.

Our annual interest amount was ₹120 crore and our earnings were never more than ₹53 crore net. The cash flow gap kept eroding the company's net worth. Despite coming from a non-finance background, Dhimant had an eye on cash flows and would often call it a reality check. When 'barter deals' were introduced to support liquidity, there was a lot of initial resistance to get these off the block. In a reasonably short time, the easing of cash flow pressure allowed us to streamline park maintenance, timely salaries, reduced outstanding in days of creditors even before we turned NPA. That is what kept the lamp burning.

# 2

# The Initial Shockwaves

*'It's just a bogus dhamki.'*

CIRCA JANUARY 2018, THE HOTEL DEAL WITH THE BILLIONAIRE had just fallen flat, but we were also in talks with other investors. One of them, Nasser, had an amazing profile. He was a suave gentleman, and we had met him sometime in 2018.

A slim man in his sixties, Nasser had salt-and-pepper hair. He was of average height and had charming manners. He always arrived elegantly dressed in a crisp white shirt and beige trousers and tan loafers. He visited Imagicaa and loved the business and greenlighted the funding from a family office in the Middle East. However, there was one hitch—the funding had to be structured through Islamic finance principles, i.e., without interest. To make it compatible with RBI rules and Indian laws, fees and equity components had to be added and structured to manage the loss of interest. The term sheet required a lot of work, as it was subject to the laws of England and fell in the London Jurisdiction—

in the Middle East, they prefer English laws for securing their interests. The two of us collaborated with a law firm to work out the finer details.

The investors were willing to provide funding to the tune of USD 264 million and wanted only 24% equity (in accordance with their lending rules). Instead of charging interest, the final term sheet provided for a small upfront fee and a heavy fee at the end of the tenure. It was a fabulous deal in monetary terms, as it allowed the lenders' outstanding amount to be paid in full and Mr Shetty continued as the majority shareholder. Not only would we salvage our reputation, but we would also have enough gunpowder left for future expansion.

We both buried ourselves in paperwork. Legal teams. Financial modelling. Clause by clause, we worked to make the impossible fit, a Middle Eastern deal stitched together inside a stressed Indian asset, shaped for international scrutiny. For the first time in months, the clouds seemed to lift.

This was the deal that could wipe the slate clean.

## Banking on Conversations

While these exciting talks were progressing, we also wanted to deter the banks from taking any drastic step till we had a firm solution to offer. Our account had now shifted to the stressed asset vertical of the banks. Mayuresh had been a part of the fundraising team, and most of the bankers in the lending branches knew him and were aware that we had a genuine project in hand, but now that we were transferred to another department, we had to build new relationships. It was definitely not easy, and we were often reminded of the importance of developing a thick skin and keep smiling. In fact, in many of these meetings, there was nothing more we could do.

The bankers in the stressed department had never met us before, and they looked at us with suspicion or viewed us as a part of the problem. Due to Mayuresh's regular interactions with lenders, we could work on potential steps that would happen next so that we could prepare some actions proactively and plan activities with words of caution or advice. Many a time we didn't really know what to do, but we often got perfect advice for what not to do, which worked well to restrict any further damage. They might let us know that some 'new' banker on the case is rigid, how to reword a specific request to make it more palatable to the consortium or what the forum would immediately refuse. These small pointers and nudges are a great help, especially when you are not allowed to plead your case in person.

In the stressed asset vertical, many of the officials we met didn't know about the project at all. It took many meetings for us to make them understand what Imagicaa was all about, our business and our assets; it was like starting from scratch every time. Seeing this enormous effort we had to put in just to give the bankers a basic understanding made us feel that banks should prioritise visits to the projects they fund so they could check and evaluate them in person. Funnily, at times we were linked to another famous troubled billionaire because of one transaction and very often had to clarify saying, 'No, we are Imagicaa, and are not a part of his empire!'

Sometimes these frustrating conversations became the fodder for our daily jokes on the world and our situation. To rephrase a line from a popular Bollywood film, 'My name is Imagicaa and I am not an ADA company.'

Both of us would go to the banks almost every alternate day to assure them that we were making all efforts to rope in investors and explore feasible options within the banking system. The conversation with Nasser was progressing well, and we were quite hopeful, but we didn't know how long the entire process would take. Interestingly though, the bankers also could not commit as to how much time they would take to get the decision on the proposals that we were submitting.

'Why do you go to the banks so often? Is anything happening?' people in the office would ask us.

In fact, at times even we felt that we and the bankers were just going through the same motions every alternate day—the two of us would head to a bank, sit down and wait till the officer called us. On some fortunate days, we would get a listening ear, but most visits were just about showing our face and barely being heard. Yet slowly, day by day, we were making some headway and started getting some positive responses from the bankers. It took months for their initial suspicion to abate and for them to start seeing us as allies. At the office though, it was difficult to explain what we were doing.

'By when?' Mr Shetty would ask us in his laconic style.

Punctuality is a hallmark of Mr Shetty, and his ability to run a project on schedule is enviable. His sharp focus, in-depth understanding and decision-making ability are excellent. Thus, having to deal with unclear responses, moving goalposts on timing and a 'file-pushing' approach were very frustrating for him. He wanted to simply get done and move on to building new concepts. Often his glare at our lack of specific dates told us that he thought little of our ability to navigate the banking system and get a closure. Sometimes Dhimant was even told, 'Bank visits won't increase footfalls, let Mayuresh handle the banks and you focus on the business.'

There was no concrete answer to give him because no banker said yes or gave us any timeline. We didn't know how long it would take for the banks to respond. The bankers also didn't know how long their committees would take. The only progress was that they started recognising us and some started seeing that we were indeed trying to find a solution.

These visits made us see that we should look at moving things piece by piece instead of going after one mega closure.

This takes us to the concept of 'seasoning of a stressed account', a concept that was explained to us by Rohit Mehta of Edelweiss. A thorough gentleman and very interesting advisor on debt resolutions, Rohit would say that for lenders to make decisions on the matter and accept a settlement value, the account needed to ripen, i.e., it needed to go through some key steps so that there would be logical steps and processes followed. They should necessarily check the boxes and have a fair rationale for the decisions they made. While we understood the concept, the process was a tough one to endure.

Later, we learnt that our regular meetings were a novel experience for most of the bank officials too. 'You guys come so regularly, we don't have to go looking for you. Most NPA accounts stop taking calls or responding. Here the CEO and CFO come and sit for hours waiting to talk to us,' one of the officials told us.

Looking back, we think personally visiting the banks and spending endless hours meeting the concerned people built trust in our intent to repay the loans and went a long way in easing some key obstacles on the way.

To balance the instructions of Mr Shetty to focus on the revenue functions as well, we used to often reach office after closing hours post the various bank visits. To the full credit of the marketing and sales team, ably led by Raveendra Singh, who relentlessly focused on the task at hand, we could have meaningful discussions and strategic outcomes almost at dinner hours!

## When Hopes Crash

While we were working out the details with a new investor and finding a common meeting ground with our bankers, an email arrived threatening us with insolvency proceedings in NCLT courts. This was barely a few days after we turned NPA. It was from RTPL (name changed), a lender who had contributed a little below 5% of the entire loan amount. This mail caught us completely unawares, because everyone we had spoken with had told us that usually lenders spend a year or so exploring a resolution before approaching the courts. We were already in talks with some investors like Nasser, which seemed to be quite positive, so we thought we had time to work things out. Now RTPL, who had contributed the least to our funds vis-à-vis other lenders, became the first lender to talk about insolvency court proceedings.

We were totally shaken up on receiving the notice because in all our lender consortium meetings, we had always been transparent with our lenders about the issues we were facing, including the cash flow gap each quarter and the ways we were trying to resolve the financial crunch. Other than flatly stating that we were in financial distress in our consortium meetings, we had revealed all pertinent details, from bank sheets to cash flows. After we turned NPA, we had been sharing information on how we planned to restructure our debt by selling our assets or going in for Prudential Framework schemes of 5/25 and S4A, which were prevalent that time. Receiving this notice despite keeping everyone informed was an enormous shock.

The National Company Law Tribunal (NCLT) was constituted under Section 408 of the Companies Act, 2013 (18 of 2013) and was operational with effect from 1 June 2016. Earlier, the restructuring and settlement of unpaid company loans that had turned into non-performing assets was managed by RBI, but after the creation of the NCLT, the power of settlement and restructuring was passed on to the judiciary.

From a company perspective, the worst scenario would be getting admitted into the NCLT proceedings and the management/board being superseded by a resolution professional, who would not know the business dynamics. In such cases, the chances of an exodus of senior personnel increase, thereby compounding the problems.

This prompt action from RTPL was even more shocking, because in 2017, when we started talks with the billionaire investor for the sale of the hotel for the partial repayment of debt, we had requested all our lenders for an NOC. For almost a year, we kept following up, but no one responded. Everyone waited for the lead banker to give the NOC before they gave theirs, as this was standard practice. We even tried requesting and reminding the lead banker about this unwritten code, and they responded with a cool, 'Why are they waiting for us. Their committees will decide for them. Who are we to tell them?' It was a frustrating merry-go-around, and we had been on it for months. Finally, after much pleading, RTPL sent a vaguely worded NOC barely four days before we turned NPA; this was many months after our initial request. Yet, barely days after we turned NPA, they threatened to take us to court without even engaging with us for a resolution.

When we received the email, we thought, 'Why have they straightaway knocked on the doors of the insolvency courts?'

At that moment, when the notice lay in front of us, the way ahead seemed bleak. We had no idea of what the future held for us. It felt like we had gone for a normal OPD check-up but had been suddenly rushed to the ICU and strapped to a ventilator. It all seemed unreal.

Till we turned into an NPA, Imagicaa had been one of RTPL's marquee projects. In fact, two years before this, RTPL's annual report had carried pictures of Imagicaa rides and restaurants—the gold rush rollercoaster and the Imagicaa capital—on the cover page. They really were glad to lend a substantial amount and had initially advanced us a loan of ₹40 crore in 2012 and then on their own initiative they topped it by 50% in 2016. We never chased them for the top-up as other banks were more than eager and in fact, we refused another lender to accommodate RTPL's disbursement. The amount of the combined loans they totally lent was possibly the maximum they were allowed to give to a single borrower as per internal norms, and they gave it to us with barely any follow-up from our end. We state this to show how surreal it felt when the lender who saw so much potential in us became the first one to drag us to courts without even engaging in a conversation.

## Sharing Bad News Is Good

Reading the mail again and again in that moment, we realised that most of our team didn't know the battles we were fighting. In fact, till Dhimant became the joint CEO of Imagicaa, he too had only a limited idea of the financial crisis because the finance team had ensured that we always had available cash flow. Of course, as a business head, he had known there was a cash crunch because in our monthly meetings we would be categorically told to get business and discussions revolved around footfalls. Yet we were never candidly told about the 'gap in finances', nor was the problem or its possible solutions ever discussed openly. Just the plain reiteration of the statement 'get more business' soon made it a routine takeaway from every monthly meeting.

Poring over RTPL's email, we foresaw that we had a long battle ahead, and we realised the need to build a clear communication channel with the senior members of the team about our finances and potential challenges ahead. The camaraderie that we shared as a team was truly a blessing. With Colonel Kale, the joint CEO and the park in-charge, Sitanshu Satapathy who headed accounts, Balanand Anand from engineering, Shivajee Sharma from operations, Veeraj Shenoy from F&B, Raveendra Singh from marketing and Vishal Sampat from retail as senior leaders, many challenges became far easier than they really were. However, we decided to conduct a meeting to share all the relevant details and break down the silo of silence around the finances.

The meeting turned out to be far more significant than we had ever imagined.

Mayuresh started by frankly detailing everything that we were doing and what the situation looked like. It was rather rare to see Mayuresh, who is usually guarded on such matters, open up and give a rather dark picture of the situation. It was the first time the gap between the business and the balance sheet was highlighted in this manner. We also openly confided in our team and told them that we both planned to see this through in whatever way we could, but if anyone in our team or any of the senior folks wanted to seek other opportunities, they were free to do so. There was no insistence that they stay—we would support their decision, as we ourselves didn't have a foolproof solution or a proper path chalked out. We wanted the team members deciding to stay to be free of any unnecessary pressure. We just told them that they shouldn't panic and resign as there was hope, but there were no answers upfront on how. More importantly, by when would things improve?

The only positive we could offer in this meeting was that despite the NPA tag and the threat of NCLT action, our business was self-sufficient and fully operational, with high-quality assets. The team effort provided an excellent guest experience and created happiness for everyone who visited Imagicaa. This silver lining did little to lighten the dark, solemn mood that had settled on everyone. While walking out of the meeting, everyone had a doomed look, as if saying, '*Ab to gayi bhains pani mein.*' Or as some felt, 'The light at the end of the tunnel turned out to be of an incoming train!'

*Intersecting Realities*

Despite the gloom that followed, we were glad that we conducted this session and shared what Imagicaa was going through. Sometimes we jokingly refer to that meeting as 'Intersecting Realities', as that is essentially what it threw up—a 'reality check'. After this meeting, we started a routine wherein we would update our senior team on what was happening every few weeks, not necessarily in a joint forum. There were numerous calls from various team members, who were all trying to take stock of the situation and understand how much time we really had.

This commitment towards communication helped build the trust in our team. Hence, four years and a pandemic later, when we succeeded in settling all our loans and removed the NPA tag from our name, most of the senior personnel were still with us. We don't think we could have stuck around together through those harrowing years of NCLT and COVID-19 had we not kept the communication channels open and frankly shared our strong sense of purpose and all that we were doing. Of course, we filtered out a few of the extremely rough and bleak moments. There were so many times when we ourselves were completely unclear as to what our fate was. We had to filter out the noise and be clear of the minute details and stayed motivated. They often say, 'Honesty is the best policy but over-disclosure is often stupidity.' We remained focused on respective areas, most importantly excelling in guest experience, asset upkeep, safety and managing creditors among others.

## Meet the Goons

Within a few days of the threatening email, we received the NCLT notice.

'It's just a bogus dhamki, an empty threat. Either ignore it or go and meet them and explain what you are doing. It will sort itself out,' we were advised.

In 2018, there were not many people who could advise us correctly on the next step to take because NCLT courts were a relatively new creature in the credit landscape of India. But the few who had some experience in debt resettlement told us that maybe RTPL was using NCLT as a threatening tool, as lenders typically tried for a resolution for a year or so, going to NCLT only when all avenues closed. Well-wishers advised us to meet the lender in person and explain the concrete steps we were undertaking to manage the situation.

On this reassurance, we quickly booked a flight to meet with the director and CFO of RTPL at their head office in Delhi.

'Where's Kapil Bagla?!' The CFO of RTPL, Hari Singh (name changed) snarled as soon as we walked in. Kapil Bagla was our former CEO. Dhimant kept quiet and let Mayuresh do the talking. Mayuresh, in turn explained how Kapil had handed over the financial responsibilities of Imagicaa to Dhimant in September 2017.

Hari Singh's anger was not soothed.

Mayuresh went on to explain how we were trying to sell our assets and about the new investors we were in talks with. 'We just need your support and patience to get us through this,' he explained. Dhimant watched the proceedings without a word, which was unlike him.

Hari Singh peremptorily brushed us aside and sent us to the waiting area, claiming that he had another meeting and would call us later. His complete disregard of the fact that we had flown in from Mumbai to discuss the matter and were trying to find a solution instead of hiding from him made Dhimant very angry. Making us sit in the lobby was clearly a pressure tactic.

'There's no meeting, I'm sure of it,' Dhimant said and purposefully crossed Hari Singh's cabin door. Through the glass walls, we could see him enjoying his lunch with two other people. Dhimant deliberately made eye contact with him to show him that he well knew what he was trying to do.

We were soon called in for a meeting with the senior director of RTPL.

'Where is that Kapil Bagla? When he needed loans, he used to come to my office, call me late at night, and now he isn't even answering my phone!' It felt like déjà vu. The same question was asked again and once more Mayuresh gave the same response to again hear that they didn't care.

'I don't want to hear all that, I want my full money.'

'Ask your promoter to put in his money,' was the next volley.

We told them that the promoter had leveraged even his own shares in Imagicaa and, due to our non-performing status, margin calls had been invoked and his stake had eroded substantially.

What does 'margin calls invoked' mean? Imagicaa had taken a ₹40-crore loan from Edelweiss, and Mr Shetty had pledged ₹90 crore worth of shares at market value in 2016. To recover the balance monies when the NCLT news broke, Edelweiss had started offloading the shares in the market, leading to a domino effect. A share that was earlier worth ₹40–45 was now trading at ₹10–12. This devaluation had brought us to our knees.

The RTPL men were not placated. 'Give us our money,' was the refrain. 'Forget the other lenders, pay us back in full and we will not only support you but also help you in crystallising settlement values with the other lenders.'

Their new line of aggression left us shocked. Even if we could somehow prioritise their repayment, it would be a breach of trust towards the other lenders. News like this doesn't remain hidden, but spreads like wildfire. A perusal of bank statements would expose it, and such an act would only add to our complications.

Sensing our refusal to take their bait, they upped their aggression levels: 'I am friends with government officials and people who matter and will ensure that they fast-track your case in NCLT. I will take your company down if this isn't understood. Talk to your promoter and let me know by tomorrow morning.'

## Planning for a Siege

Back in Mumbai, we felt utterly dejected. It seemed like a trip in futility. We were now quite unsure of how to proceed. As we replayed the entire trip in our minds, the apathy of the lender who was trying to blackmail us made us furious. This treatment from the lender and their approach was something we had never experienced in our careers of over two decades.

We had always loved the challenges and a unique platform Imagicaa gave us. Many of us felt fortunate and grateful for this amazing opportunity. Moreover, there were no structures or pre-decided processes or systems that we could emulate, as it was the first project in the country at such scale. Now, as we grumbled against the treatment we had just received, we realised Imagicaa had once again given us yet another opportunity. Whether we would be able to deliver on it remained to be seen, but we were both ready to give it our all and prepared to be even the last men standing. No one understood the history and dynamics behind the loan and Imagicaa better than us, and we thought we were the only ones who could do something about it.

Imagicaa was a dream that employed more than 1,500 people, and neither of us needed any discussion to decide on the simple fact that we would not let this dream go without a good fight. We always knew that the two of us would stand by each other in these times, no matter what. A strong belief in the concept of Imagicaa made us hopeful of a successful revival. Our simultaneous focus was to maintain park assets in the best possible condition, employees motivated and the guest experience to be of the highest order no matter what. This of course came with the goal that the situation should be win-win for all stakeholders.

One of the most common answers we got whenever we asked people about how we should proceed was, '*Pehle NCLT admit ho jaate toh aaj settle kar sakte the*...' If you had gone to NCLT first, you would be settling the case now.

Why should we have got admitted to NCLT earlier? It had seemed right to us to try our best to pay our dues while we could.

But more experienced people opined that every time we scrounged around and paid our interest somehow, we were emptying out our future war chest. We were told that if we had declared ourselves as NPA earlier, then we could have saved that money and used it in the final settlement pay-outs. Plus, that war chest money could have added weight to some of our decisions when the time came for resolution.

This answer obviously offered no solutions. We could not turn back the clock.

'What can we do now?' we asked.

Nobody had any concrete answers, just opinions or anecdotes from the experiences of others.

The two of us started gathering these small yet critical pieces of information because we didn't plan to go easily into the night.

*Amigo Mantra #5: Corporate encounters—meeting wolves in business suits.*

*Amigo Mantra #6: Legacy is of no use when it's time for recovery!*

# Thought #2: Navigating NCLT

After returning from our unsuccessful discussion with RTPL, we started speaking to lawyers and asking how best we could manage this situation.

Everyone we spoke to bluntly told us that if somebody files a case in NCLT against a company, then the natural tendency of the court will be to accept that the company is a defaulter and admit it under NCLT. The simple fact is that you cannot deny a default in the payment of interest beyond a point. A company's default is usually in black and white, and the purpose of the NCLT is to find a judiciary way of making a turnaround or a recovery. Thus, in the NCLT process, the natural tendency of the court is to accept the default and admit a company into NCLT.

## What Happens to a Company in the NCLT Process

Businesses are brought to the NCLT court when one or more of their lenders or creditors file a case against them in court for non-payment of dues, there are issues of major mismatch of plan vs actuals, mismanagement, or when a company wants to wind down.

The NCLT aims to provide holistic solutions to the following issues:

- What happens when a company goes bankrupt or stops servicing its loans?
- What happens when the promoters want to wind down a company?
- What happens in cases of mismanagement?
- How will the recovery proceeds be apportioned among the eligible stakeholders i.e. primarily secured lenders, creditors, employees?

Most professionals have learnt how to start or grow a company; they are well-versed with the ideas and strategies of growth and expansion. But very few know what actually happens when a company goes through NCLT. These are subjects no one usually talks about until they face such a situation. There is a certain amount of stigma attached to professionals who are going through this process or have navigated it. Sometimes, many learned professionals and even entrepreneurs perceive this as a taboo. They are often viewed negatively by fellow professionals and colleagues, and people instinctively think of them as a part of the problem and sometimes as panauti—carrying bad luck.

Dhimant says, 'On a more personal note, since as the KMP, or key managerial personnel, of a company which was categorised as an NPA, I could not close a personal joint bank account with my wife. This realisation hit me hard, but thanks to my considerate wife, the shock was buffered. At Imagicaa too, a few employees resigned because of their fear of NCLT proceedings. Some feared they would be summoned in court. One employee wanted to buy a house and thought his home loan would not get sanctioned and another employee in our marketing department said he was given no option, as his father found a more "stable company" by signing up on job portals himself. I always wished them well because everyone did what best they could in their circumstances; it was an unknown minefield for all of us.

'In one such incident, a neighbour from my residential society, when he heard about my visits to court and the overall situation, made a stinging remark: "Why do you have to do such a thing that you have to land up in the courts? Maybe you should rethink!"

'In another incident, a college friend's eleven-year-old son, who happens to be a buddy of my younger son quizzed me about the financial status of our company in a *chai pe charcha* get-together, where twenty of us were present, including my sons. Moreover, he was probably worried about his friend, whose father was maybe not getting salaries regularly, I guess. I froze and felt bewildered, thinking of all that his young mind was imagining. Just think of the impact such a situation can have on young ones.

'In another incident, the mother of my son's classmate gave me a perplexed look when they heard that I work for Imagicaa. Her husband was a financial consultant himself. She asked my wife if there was any financial crisis at home and was curious to know more. My wife responded with a smile and a simple shrug to end the conversation.

'So, some out of concern, some out of curiosity and some out of innocence, we received many such questions and comments through that period. It is very important that communication at home be handled well and transparently. Also important is to have a financial cushion, keeping each one's criteria and goals in mind.

'My wife is mentally very strong and is a real minimalist. The home front was in the safest pair of hands, so the dark clouds of NCLT couldn't affect me much. I could be fully focused on debt resolution and turnaround matters.'

## What You Can Expect

The biggest learning for us was to understand that NCLT is a process and a journey, more of a marathon than a sprint. You don't have to be the fastest but need grit and endurance to survive. Being summoned to NCLT court doesn't mean that your business will be immediately shut down. NCLT has various steps and stages, and many details need to be clearly understood. Usually the secured lenders' claims get prioritised, and they too do not receive their full dues. There is method to it, so one needs to go through the motions.

Thus, panicking or closing your mind and trying to pre-empt problems isn't the way to go. Worst of all is to lose calm and react, which can cause collateral damage to others around you more than yourself. Also, like in cricket, you have to focus on the ball carefully and not keep looking at the scoreboard. Runs aren't going to come by just like that; you need to focus on each delivery as if it is the most important thing in the world at that time. No point thinking about it once crossed—start focusing on the next one.

Only when the NCLT court is satisfied that the resolution plan approved by the committee of creditors meets its requirements does it approve the plan. Before that the company executive powers are handed over to an Interim Resolution Professional (IRP) or a Resolution Professional (RP).

The role of the RP is akin to that of a turnaround specialist. It may turn into the role of a liquidator as well, depending on the complexity and business situation of the company. They take over the entire management and operation of the insolvent corporate in the name of the creditors. The board of directors or the management becomes null and void. The RP can sell the assets for scrap to pay off the creditors, if there is no acceptable resolution plan in sight and no buyer for all the assets of the company.

For an employee, it means that their ultimate boss changes, and they report to the court-appointed RP.

For Imagicaa, it could mean the end of a dream. We knew how much juggling we had to do to keep the juggernaut of India's biggest entertainment park rolling. Our work went beyond handling manpower, looking after engineering and maintenance, creating marketing campaigns, keeping the e-commerce engine running, managing safety and maintaining excellent standards of service while balancing seasonality and the local ecosystem. We knew an RP may not be able to manage this scope, especially since their mandate would be very different and unique. Unlike a regular manufacturing or a real estate project, getting admission in NCLT would possibly be a slow poison for the business.

# 3

# The Road to Salvation?

*'Gone, gone, gone … now forget it, nothing is going to happen … straight to NCLT!'*

THE TALKS WITH NASSER'S FUND HOUSE WERE LOOKING GOOD. We went through four to five rounds of term sheets. It was a great deal, and we were very excited about it. Dhimant and Mayuresh had several rounds of discussion around this. Although Mayuresh hadn't met Nasser in person, both Mr Shetty and Dhimant were very gung-ho about him and the overall proposal. It simply would have put us on a path of growth and accelerated expansion, leaving stress far behind. Nasser was an investment banker who managed investments of a powerful and a large family of the Middle East.

If we cracked this, leave aside the dark, it would be all sunshine ahead. Amidst the NCLT cloud, he seemed to be our white knight. Discussions were progressing well and the well-structured MoU we received had the potential of putting Imagicaa on the growth track.

The main issue at that time, *though we didn't view it as an issue then*, was that we only spoke to Nasser. Everything was relayed to us through Nasser, and he communicated all our responses. After nearly three months of engagement, we tentatively agreed on a date of travel to Dubai to sign the finalised term sheet. When we were looking to book tickets and manage other logistics, we called Nasser for a confirmation of the date and time of the meeting.

We got no response.

This was an unusual eerie silence, because Nasser was always very prompt in his responses. We kept trying for days. He was unreachable by phone or by mail.

Even if he wanted to back out at this stage, he could always do it through a formal and crisp communication. He was very clinical and could convey his thoughts articulately without hurting anyone's feeling. We were at a loss to understand what was happening.

Mayuresh, as usual, turned sleuth and started looking for clues. He went over all our conversations and started checking the net.

After a few weeks, a Google search revealed that a man named Nasser had been killed in a robbery attempt in a five-star Dubai hotel.

Could it be the same Nasser?

There was a rumour going around at the time that due to a change in regime in a neighbouring Middle Eastern country, the people who had been managing funds of opposition families were being targeted. Was Nasser a victim of such an attack?

To investigate further, Dhimant visited Dubai to see if he could be contacted in some way, or if there was someone who knew him at his address. While he could locate the company name and details, the operations seemed to have wound up. While checking with the security guards, Dhimant was told that recently there was a closure—beyond that, there was no information. Finally, after weeks of follow-up and hopeful waiting, we had to concede defeat. We had no concrete idea of what had gone wrong, only theories. Nasser was one of the few gentlemen we met in these years and what actually happened to him is still a mystery to us. We will never truly know. We lost a gentleman, along with a potential deal.

During the same time, Ajay Sharma (name changed), a financial intermediary who seemed more like a bouncer from some night club, with his thick moustache and peculiar attire, was introduced to us through a new employee in our internal audit department named Mishra. Mishra came to us with promises of interest rates as low as 3–5%. We were taken aback at these low rates, as whoever we had spoken to until then, from ARCs to fund houses, all demanded 18–24% returns on their investments (IRR) along with equity. It didn't seem realistic, and we shrugged off his suggestions, but he kept on talking to us about these rates and what a great opportunity we were missing out on. After much cajoling by Mishra, we spoke to Ajay Sharma, and he also quoted such low funding rates. Such a rate seemed impossible, more so because of our default credit rating.

'Who on the earth gives such low rates to NPA companies? Have you gone mad? *Yeh marvayange*!' exclaimed Arvind, a finance teammate in his usual grandfatherly tone.

It smelt of a scam all over, but Mr Shetty often told us, 'We should evaluate it thoroughly till such time we that we don't cross out the option as long as it can increase the recovery of the lenders and if it is through lawful means. It is our responsibility to do our best, and sometimes you may have to go beyond the call of duty, but try it.' Possibly this philosophy stemmed from trying to do the right thing even in the face of a lack of choices in this grim scenario. We had internally articulated it as Principle of 1% Hope. We gave in to our curiosity and agreed to a meeting with Ajay Sharma and an experienced so-called 'fundraiser'.

As we walked in for the meeting in the lobby of the Sahara Star restaurant Casa Blanca near Mumbai Airport, Ajay met us with an added swagger because the CEO of the company that would facilitate the funding had come for the meeting. As soon as we met, Ajay proclaimed, 'I'm helping you out. *Tum to defaulter ho* (you're a defaulter), and I have a solution that will solve your problem. Why did you take so long to respond to Mishra?'

The CEO, on the other hand, was obviously a far more measured personality in comparison to Ajay. He just shared the finer details and kept to business.

'You first have to obtain a letter of credit and then later cancel it,' he told us.

'But we are not traders,' we said. 'We cannot do this. Trading companies might do this. We are a project company.'

'You can. I'll explain how.'

As he started to explain, we realised this scheme was not only smelling wrong, it was all wrong. We were aghast at the ease with which this was explained.

Their scheme ran thus—a company places an order in India to buy something from a place in Middle East like Dubai or Doha or Hong Kong and a contract is created with another entity. Against that contract, a banker gives the company a bank guarantee or a letter of credit (LC) from a reputed bank to secure the payment. The company then uses that LC or guarantee and goes to another domestic or international lender to raise money against it at a very low cost. Open one LC, open a second LC, close the first LC, open a third LC, close the second LC ... and so on, repeated indefinitely.

We had one simple question: 'Even if we get that money, how do we repay it when the six-to-twelve-month period ends? What happens to the goods?'

That's when he revealed the extent of the fishiness of the plan, 'Before the goods come to India, we will place another order from say Hong Kong, and we'll do a similar transaction! You can keep on repeating this and repay the earlier ones ...'

Basically, the CEO was talking about creating fictitious transactions. We bluntly told him that we were absolutely not interested in this. It was a clear violation of the Foreign Exchange Management Act (FEMA) and an unscrupulous practice. In Hindi, it was a *topi ghoomao* transaction without a *topi*.

Seeing us walk away from this brilliant idea, Ajay angrily stood up and said, '*Tumhara* TADA (sic) *aur ye sab kya hota hai*. (What is your TADA and all this?) You don't have to do anything, we'll handle all the documentation. *Aaj shaam tak ka time deta hoon, decide karlo. Doob jaoge warna.*' (We're giving you time till this evening to decide. You'll sink otherwise.)

In his anger, he mixed up TADA and FEMA. Maybe he never knew the difference between the two.

We walked out laughing after this episode.

Ajay called Dhimant late in the night and yelled at him. 'You are responsible for your company's misfortune. Better understand what I am offering you.' When Dhimant didn't respond apart from an uncharacteristic silence, he slammed the phone down.

The main lesson we learnt from this was that when anyone gives you a deal that's too good to be true, it probably is—either fake or fraudulent. It is an age-old lesson, but time and again we need to go through it till we learn it fully. Even then, it needs reminding so that we don't fall for it, regardless of how true it is made to sound.

*Amigo Mantra #7:* Chai se zyada ketli garam! *Those who unduly flaunt their importance should be handled tactfully.*

*Amigo Mantra #8:* Jab ho saamne farzi insaan, chalta nahin koi gyan! *When faced with a fake person, intelligent arguments are futile.*

## Trying to Right a Wrong

One big thing that was bothering us beyond the NPA status and NCLT case was that we had lost the trust of a reputed person, i.e. the billionaire investor. In good faith, the gentleman had made a sizeable deposit of earnest money in Imagicaa, but when the hotel sale deal got cancelled following complications arising from the land litigation, we were unable to pay him back. It was a black mark that we wanted to erase from our names at any cost. We would often talk about it. In one of the discussions with their ultra conservative lawyer, Dhimant suggested they participate in the entire transaction and gain multiple benefits instead of trying to solve this problem. The next day, Dhimant hit upon a fabulous structure that we could adopt for the transaction. When we excitedly told Mr Shetty about it, he, in his characteristic style, shrugged it off. It took several meetings and a lot of cajoling for him to reluctantly do what we requested. Mr Shetty approached Jash Shah (name changed), with whom he occasionally played tennis at his club.

Jash was a very high-profile owner of a broking house, and he was closely connected to the billionaire investor. In fact, Jash was the one who had introduced us to the investor. When the deal got cancelled, Jash too felt a sense of moral responsibility because of the pending earnest money deposit. Based on our requests, the new deal was finally offered to the billionaire investor—Imagicaa in its entirety instead of a part transaction. Fortunately, the new deal interested Jash, because it gave him a chance to change the narrative and subsume the advance and of course presented a much larger opportunity for this marquee investor.

Jash's team soon got to work. Around five analysts were put on our project, and they interrogated us in detail because they were categorically told by Jash, '*Kal mujey kuch bhi business key barey mey kuch poochna hai*, I will ask only you guys and not anyone else.' If he ever wanted to know anything about the business, they would be the ones he would ask.

Jash also got a new lawyer for this deal. The billionaire investor's ultra conservative lawyer was someone Dhimant would call 'opinion impaired'. A good lawyer should be able to identify the merits of a case and give their view, which this man didn't seem to be capable of. Anybody could tell that there was litigation concerning that land, but a good lawyer would have analysed the merits of the case and given a directional view instead of choosing to stop engaging altogether. It's far easier to not do something that looks slightly difficult than check to see if there was any substance to the case at all. Having to deal with a different lawyer was a welcome change.

At the end of a few intense months, which had the two of us constantly answering questions, digging out details and showcasing Imagicaa, the lawyer and the analysts both gave Jash a positive signal. Jash's genuine concern was that we would leave after having gone through this 'ordeal', as he benevolently termed it. He called us one Sunday afternoon to check whether we were ready to stay on in Imagicaa after the investor took over.

A thousand times yes! An absolute affirmative! When we had remained in the worst times, why would we think of leaving when things were better?

After that conversation and the positive go-ahead from the analyst, things sped up.

The investor now agreed to pump in ₹735 crore into Imagicaa because the intensive analysis and due diligence had revealed the potential of the business to the investor and his team. The additional money would serve to increase footfalls and add new rides, concepts and a budget hotel. For strategic investors like them, debt settlement is not a great way of parking their money; they came in for the growth prospects, which a business has to exhibit to attract such investors.

Once all these details were smoothened out, the two of us were surprisingly dropped from the conversation, which now continued between Mr Shetty and the investment bankers. We later came to know that closed-door discussions had taken place, which we should have ideally been called for, but weren't.

The two of us went back to handling regular queries from Jash's team, meeting bankers and attending NCLT hearings. After a month, the calls suddenly stopped. We checked with Mr Shetty if he knew the reason behind this, but got no clear response.

Later, after much digging, we learnt that in one of his private talks with Jash, Mr Shetty had indicated his interest in a small parcel of Imagicaa's land to do a joint development (which wasn't even contiguous with the park land). He wanted it to be kept out of the transaction. Being a man of few words, he didn't reveal that the reason behind this was to honour a promise he had made a few years ago to a real-estate developer to open an old-age home or an affordable housing project on that land. He simply assumed that in a transaction of this size, this plot would be insignificant. Jash agreed to this carve-out in principle, but when the investment bankers were informed of this request, they sniffed a potential concern, and this led to a complete trust deficit in Jash's mind. To clarify this hypothesis, Jash had proposed an impromptu pre-deal inspection at Imagicaa, very close to the purported signing date.

Jash, his investment banker, a few of his team members and the two of us were on the terrace of the hotel in Imagicaa. We had a bird's eye view of the entire property. Jash pointed to that part of land and the architect spoke effusively about it, imagining a different utilisation. As Jash had the financial muscle to back more development, he could possibly offer his architectural services. A glance passed between Jash and his investment banker. The meeting ended cordially, but after that day, every communication stopped.

We had got it wrong the first time because of the litigation. This time we ticked all the boxes and worked a lot harder, but the above 'side conversation' acted like fuel on nascent doubts and derailed the entire process.

This is something we never could understand—why is there any need to break the continuity and momentum in such critical transactions? New elements to these vital conversations further aggravate the situation, having zero background of what has transpired so far and the reasons behind them. This was a case of working in silos, and that is what prevented the execution of the deal.

Life would have been so different had that deal happened. By June 2019, our NPA status had crossed one year, the RTPL case against us in NCLT was moving ahead and one more lender was gearing up to file a petition against us in NCLT. Things quickly started turning more uncertain.

## The Funding Stories

Scathed by the effect of the land litigation on potential buyers and investors, we had become more cautious in our dealings. To be doubly transparent and to avoid this matter coming up later as a due diligence point, we now began all our discussions with new investors by being very upfront about the litigation.

When we explained our situation to Rahul Manwani (name changed), the young and confident country head of a well-known fund house headquartered in the US that also had a decent-sized APAC office, he seemed quite unperturbed and ready to do business with us. In fact, he said that his fund house was already funding a project where there was some litigation and that they had found a business case for it. Our case seemed no different to him, prima facie. We sensed that it was the opportunity in adversity that he wanted to seize.

Armed with this confidence, a meeting was fixed with Rahul, Mr Shetty, and the two of us. It all sounded good, but as in the deal with the billionaire investor, after getting the transaction to a certain level, we were again left out of the picture at a key stage, and the meetings continued with Mr Shetty. Later, we came to know from Mr Shetty that Rahul's fund house had said that they would be ready to invest ₹650 crore.

The quoted number was a big jump from the number that was going around in the market. At that time, another asset reconstruction company, Zeon (name changed) was also interested in investing in Imagicaa and were actively discussing the purchase. However, their offer was significantly lower at ₹450 crore. And this was after conducting a few rounds of due diligence and putting a zillion conditions on Mr Shetty.

For legal due diligence, Zeon appointed a big law firm. There was also a commercial due diligence which looked at the validity and future assessments of the numbers. Someone pointed out that they would also need technical due diligence for the machinery and the rollercoasters. There was no rollercoaster or similar high-end theme park equipment valuer in India, so they sought overseas help.

Rahul never conducted any full-fledged due diligence before making his offer. But his confidence, air of professionalism and of course the backing of a big fund reassured us, so we had no reason to question anything. All the boxes were ticked, we thought, so what was the need for it? We saw it as a gentleman's word.

## Finding the Right Numbers

Valuations depend a lot on the investors' perspective, their views on perceived opportunities and threats. Investors would try and ring-fence themselves from any unknown liabilities or risks and of course maintain their own parameters of return on investments (ROI) numbers. Essentially, a sustainable number from their parameters is offered as a settlement value to lenders and the unsustainable value is termed as 'haircut'. It is a big number game, and nobody wants to quote a higher number to the banks because a 'good deal' usually means a high margin of comfort. Zeon's standpoint throughout our arguments for quoting the low amount of ₹450 crore for a ₹1,020 crore loan was, 'If we get it cheaper, then why not? Also, what if there are some unknown risks, variables that we don't know today? And we are assuming so many risks too. Also, the pressure on your business to deliver would be less in case of lower capital deployed in settlement.'

The professional funds are champion number crunchers. When they want to buy an asset from the banks, they want it at the lowest possible rate and imagine the bleakest scenarios, but internally, of course, they have high numbers in their analysis. That's why when Rahul Manwani's quote came, we felt it was transactable and seemed like a practical, deal-making approach.

Mr Shetty was quite gung-ho about the deal with Rahul. It met his objectives to return greater value back to the lenders. Ironically, he'd never taken a loan for any of his earlier ventures, and the first loan he took turned into an NPA. Maybe he felt that this deal gave him an opportunity to demonstrate in action to the banks that he was earnest about paying them back. Dhimant had his doubts, mainly because there was nothing in writing with Rahul. No formal term sheet had been signed with his fund house. We also felt that it was better to quote a slightly lower number to the banks so that if there were some diligence gaps or lender negotiations in the future, we had some space to manoeuvre and at least bring positive closure.

Before the meeting with the leading bank chairman, the two of us tried to reason with Mr Shetty that while we had a sincere intention to pay the highest possible amount to the banks, we needed to keep some headroom for negotiations. The multiple levels within the banks coupled with the entire consortium or the committee to negotiate, so a buffer would help sweeten the deal. But he insisted we quote the full amount to the banks. Mayuresh had already drafted two documents, one quoting ₹650 crore and another with the lower number of ₹600 crore. We gave both to him just before the meeting and requested him to show only the ₹600 crore one. He smiled as he took the papers but, to our utter dismay, did just the opposite.

As expected, the bankers were very happy with Rahul's number because it beat Zeon's offer of ₹450 crore by a large margin. With Rahul's offer, the banks felt that they would get more than 50% return on their loan amount. It seemed like a great deal, especially since in most NPA cases, the recovery rate is less than 40%, some even at 16–17%.

## Auction Plan

Based on these discussions, the banks started the well-defined auction process. Banks take around four to five months to roll out an auction (conversely, it took them six months to move ahead on an NOC which would have avoided an NPA altogether).

Once the auction was announced, there was a flutter in the industry, and the appointed process advisor for the auction received about fifteen expressions of intent. Officially, we were never informed of the identity of the bidders because the protocol is that interested parties mail the bank their queries, which the banks redirect to us for our responses. However, many of them reached out for some clarification on the nature of our business and to understand the existing litigation. Unlike Zeon, Jash and the other fund houses that we personally met and engaged with earlier, the bidders for auctions get a defined time frame to understand the business potential and complete their due diligence from the virtual data room. Since we didn't know who had made expressions of interest (EOI), we couldn't approach them, but we did our best to explain the details to those who reached out.

As the day of the auction dawned, we were quite excited to imagine the end of our NPA journey. We had more than one contender, and the banks had planned an open online auction with the method of price discovery, which meant that there was no reserve price. There was nothing to limit the buyers to put their bid on.

As the minutes ticked past, we waited.

Out of over a dozen expressions of intent, only two bidders submitted their bank guarantees and became eligible for joining the bid window and then … nothing.

There was no bid. Not even one at ₹400 or ₹450 crore.

Not ONE bid.

Bankers soon started calling us and asking why the interested funds were not bidding. It was a terrible moment for the bankers—they had planned the auction after convincing their boards about the bidders and the assured bid of ₹650 crore based on the word of Rahul Manwani and Mr Shetty's word to the lenders. They could not now explore solutions outside the bankruptcy courts without losing face. There would now be a domino effect on fallen expectations, and it was an utterly embarrassing moment for all.

The trust we had worked so hard to build with the bankers came crashing down. We even went to meet one of our bankers, but he was utterly distraught because at that moment he was being called by his seniors to explain this debacle. While rushing off for his uncomfortable meeting, he screamed, '*Gaya, gaya, gaya … ab bhool jao, kuch nahin hone wala hai … seedha NCLT!*' (Gone, gone, gone … now forget it, nothing is going to happen … straight to NCLT!)

Neither of us had any witty repartee as we watched him go. NCLT loomed larger than ever before in our minds.

We realised that we had to find a solution for our bankers because we needed their ongoing support while working through the NPA process. In the last three hours of the bid, we presented a company offer of ₹575 crore through our investment banker. It was a back-up proposal that the banker had worked out. In that offer, we planned to sell some park properties like the hotel and land and raise high-cost debt to reach that amount. But at that moment, the bankers were very angry and not interested in that offer. It was one of the few times we were at the bottom quartile of possibilities, lower than the 1% hope.

Later, when the dust had settled, we met and asked the fund houses why they didn't bid. After all, there was a clear business case, and they had requisite approvals, especially Zeon. Officially, we were met with complete silence on that issue, but a few pointers came our way. It's human nature to ascribe higher value to something when we see another person interested in it. On the other hand, everyone wants to avoid the winner's curse—the tendency for the winning bid to exceed the worth of an item.

In an auction, especially for an NPA company that operated in a niche most were not familiar with, no one wanted to be the first to bid. If this was a manufacturing company, it would have been easier. Many experts would have been able to put a value to it. Imagicaa was difficult to put a price to for most of them, because it is a one-of-its-kind park in India and had its own opportunities and challenges.

The interested bidders stayed their hand and waited for the others to reveal their quote so that they could confirm if their quote was anywhere near what the others were thinking.

It was a waiting game, and no one blinked.

Even the ₹575 crore that we offered to the banks was a realistic number. However, it came at a very wrong time. Timing matters in numbers and such transactions. In fact, we now believe that only the timing and how it plays out in other people's minds matters—the perception of that number at that point of time.

Valuation numbers are not written in stone, and some experts say that valuation is a craft and not really an art or science. A number that people might not like at a certain time might become the best option later.

Looking back, we can say that we truly experienced what that quote meant. Going through this sequence of disasters left us reeling. Even the maxims and jokes we said to each other became a little dark. The banter was toned down and more solemn now. The only thing that kept us going through this time was our shared belief.

> *Amigo Mantra #9: It ain't over till it's over.*
>
> *Amigo Mantra #10:* Dushkalat terhava mahina (Marathi proverb). *The year of a famine always appears to have thirteen months. Troubles don't follow laws of magnetism, but attract more of their kind!*

# Thought #3: What Fund Houses Look For

The fund houses that participate in stressed assets basically look at the earning potential of the company they bid for. They want the answer to one question: Can this asset make money?

During our presentations, we faced one major stumbling block. The three-million-footfall projection was well known in most financial circles. Like the photo of a prospective bride or groom, our proposal had been widely circulated in the financial circles and had been seen by almost all credible potential investors and investment bankers. A theme park is a business in which everyone can give you advice, just like any cricket fan can have an opinion on how Dhoni or Virat or Rohit should have played on some day! Many would look at the earlier projections and our actual numbers and pass the verdict that the fault lay in the marketing. Often our discussions would veer off in a completely different tangent and we would get advice on how we should market our park well.

'Why don't you put up your ads on the hoardings around Bandra–Worli Sea Link? That will get you more eyeballs and eventually footfalls,' advised one of the Zeon partners.

'You are charging very little for your tickets. You should charge at least ₹5000 per ticket. We pay more than that for Disneyland,' advised Jash Shah.

Mr Shetty would often remark with a smirk that everyone knows our business better than us. Time and again we would have to explain all our efforts in marketing and sales. How many cities we'd tried, our team size, pricing formula, how much discounting should we do—all these points were examined and dissected by many of the fund houses who had brilliant people on board. However, these same people had no experience in running parks, managing their ecosystems and facing the inbound leisure tourism challenges of Maharashtra. In fact, Imagicaa had had some of the brightest minds in marketing and sales since its inception. They had built a very strong brand but always fell short of this magic number of 3 million. We had the highest staff turnover in this department while we were solving a completely different problem than what we should have had in the very first place.

After hearing many such suggestions with no connection to the ground reality, Dhimant would often ruefully laugh and exclaim, 'Nothing is impossible for the one who isn't doing it!' The famous phrase 'think why not' kept hitting us like tidal waves, and the person who reasons otherwise is seen lacking a positive approach or the imagination to achieve success!

Zeon had even identified a replacement for Dhimant before the acquisition! One day, Mr Shetty, with his trademark smile, looked at us and said that Zeon had headhunted a person as the new CEO and showed us his picture. Dhimant was bewildered but hid his disconcertment with a chuckle and with a cup of tea in his hand, responded, 'We'll see when the deal is done with Zeon. First, let's resolve the problem at hand!'

In this whole process, the two of us interacted with five or six large fund houses. Speaking with fund houses is not an easy task. They are very intensive in their scrutiny and analysis and spend a minimum of one or two months discussing and understanding the deal from all angles—legal, financial, technical and of course commercial.

Fund houses are good options for funding, but they don't provide an easy exit for promoters with the number of representations, warranties, indemnifications and the list just goes on. In fact, experienced people say that sometimes distressed fund investors could be a case of 'from the frying pan to the fire' for the promoters and the old employees. Especially in our case, where a change of promoter was happening at the behest of the lenders as opposed to a regular sale, where proceeds do not go to an outgoing promoter.

In our case, Zeon wanted us to indemnify certain liabilities, including the land litigation, and of course give them a majority share in the company, while Rahul Manwani's fund house wanted a commitment to mandatorily sell certain assets and a shareholding equal to Mr Shetty's.

Post the auction debacle, we also spoke with top fund houses like Carlyle, Blackstone, Brookfield, ANA Capital, Aion, etc. During these discussions, one of the fund houses wanted greater than 74% share and wanted to delist, while another wanted to create a complicated structure with the park, hotel and land and some wanted larger size of transaction as we didn't fit into their threshold of transaction size. If any of the deals with the fund houses had gone through, Mr Shetty would have had very uncomfortable and unreasonable commitments to honour.

Our learnings from interacting with these fund houses were immense. Especially Carlyle, where their India-focused stressed accounts senior partners Merrill Goulding and Ian Thomson flew down specially to visit the park and spent an entire day and real quality time with us to understand the business and displayed amazing humility. In complete contrast, the MD of a large global stressed fund showed unbounded arrogance and wanted to make sweeping changes without a discussion or even a prior situational analysis. His behaviour reeked of the arrogance of money. In a third such case, a partner assumed responsibility for our marketing and began making suggestions that only a novice would do. The more people we met, we got a sense that this was not just about financial restructuring but about finding the right entity in whose hands the company would thrive as a consumer business. Kiran Chonkar of BDO (they were Process Advisors in the auction, appointed by lenders) had given us this advice during our first auction process: we needed to figure out who was a serious buyer and thereafter not to go fishing around for better deals, as it could end up derailing the one on hand. His experience dealing with various resolutions (handling an assortment of lenders) and promoters (entrepreneurs, with varied philosophies) and therefore the complexities involved, was worth gold. Such nuggets of wisdom were very precious and helped us make right efforts and decisions. As they say, life is a summation of decisions and one can only figure when you connect the dots backwards!

# 4

# A Case of Skill and Time

*'You will be fined ₹50,000!'*

After talks with our lender RTPL came to a dead end because they were unwilling to even explore a feasible resolution or give us time, we realised we had no option but to fight it out in the courts and avoid NCLT. This was the only way to save the company and realise the best possible value for the lenders. By now, we were told that given the unique nature of our assets, the value would be highest when the assets were well maintained and cash accretive. During these times, we also found some pundits from the finance world who would tell Mr Shetty to shut the park and let the lenders come to the table for a resolution. Notably, a large workforce from a local catchment was dependent on our operations. We tried in our best capacity to maintain the social fabric and prioritised the people and park assets.

On 30 January 2019, a few months before our failed auction, Mayuresh went for our first NCLT court hearing. We were unsure of what to expect. Our lawyers told us that this was supposed to be a routine hearing—they would present the case in court and ask for time to review as it was the first date for the matter.

The law firm had not yet appointed a senior counsel, so a junior lawyer represented us. We later discovered that this is the norm in most cases and, even after appointing the senior lawyer, law firms check if you want the senior lawyer to represent you at a particular hearing or if a junior lawyer would do. The commercials for both are obviously very different.

The firm later informed us that the judge who would be presiding on the particular bench where our matter had got listed was A. Rawat (name changed). Of course, the name meant nothing to us, as we were complete newbies in this vortex.

When our case number got called out, our young lawyer got up and requested for an extension as planned.

'Extension? You had two weeks and now you are saying you need more time?' the sharp-eyed, seasoned judge snapped angrily, glaring at the rookie over his metal-framed glasses.

Our lawyer immediately went on the back foot and started apologising, 'Sir … uh your lordship. I am very sorry. This matter came to us recently …'

The judge was not placated by this response. In fact, his anger kept mounting and he declared that he would fine us ₹50,000!

Mayuresh was sitting right behind our lawyer and wanted to stand up and speak but worried that by interrupting court proceedings, he might make matters worse. Seeing our lawyer almost beg for an extension made him anxious, and the mere concept of a penalty added to that anxiety. It wasn't the amount that was concerning, but the fact that the penalty becomes a part of the court record. When any other judge would open our case, they would read the previous records and on seeing a penalty, they might automatically form an unfavourable impression of our case. We didn't want that.

Our young lawyer continued apologising profusely, but Judge Rawat seemed to be in no mood to relent. He was going to dictate the penalty to his clerk when without any ceremony, abruptly, he got up and left! It was so sudden that we were all caught unawares.

In those precious minutes while the judge was away, a senior lawyer stepped in and spoke to our lawyer. We don't know what he said, but our lawyer regained some of his composure.

As soon as the judge returned and resumed the proceedings, our lawyer pleaded once again with the judge and said, 'Your lordship, please don't penalise my client for my mistake on their very first hearing.'

This somehow seemed to placate the judge.

He relented and didn't impose the penalty on us and even granted us the extension. The change was so drastic that it seemed like a miracle!"

Later, we found out the reason for the miracle. Martyr's Day is celebrated on 30 January to mark the day of Mahatma Gandhi's assassination. At 11 a.m. every 30 January, the judges in court congregate and observe two minutes of silence. Our judge had left to observe silence for two minutes as a mark of respect and that silence had worked its magic in an unimaginable way.

The two of us discussed the happenings in court once Mayuresh returned. We had decided that we would not work in silos but keep each other fully informed of what was happening. Dhimant immediately called up Senior Advocate Sanjay Asher, the head of the law firm we were working with, and strongly urged that our case be given importance and escalated. There had been a near miss, which we could ill afford. We evidently needed a senior counsel who would be able to steer the discussions and argue with experience. After hearing Dhimant out, our law firm Crawford Bayley directed us to Advocate Prateek Seksaria.

'*Achha abhi batao kya hai*?' (So tell me, what is the matter?) was the first question Prateek Seksaria asked us.

Prateek didn't carry himself like the power-punching senior counsels we saw in movies, nor the ones with salt-and-pepper hair with serious and stiff suits we met earlier. He came across like the man next door, friendly, in a relaxed shirt, with twinkling eyes that seemed to X-ray you with a lazy grace and a cool intelligence. It was rather hard to predict in the first meeting what kind of a lawyer he would be.

In our first meeting, we didn't know how to proceed. At that moment, we could not picture Prateek and more so, not even begin to imagine that behind this understated attitude lay a powerful personality that could easily dominate heated courtroom arguments. We just trusted Sanjay Asher (of Crawford Bayley) and took on Prateek as our senior counsel. It was a recommendation we are forever grateful for.

## Saving the Day

Around the time of our first auction we received a very strange invite one day. A financial consultant we knew named Imtiaz Siddiqui (name changed) told us that the *opposing* party's senior counsel wanted to meet us in his chambers.

Nothing good is going to come out of this, we thought, but it was very difficult to ignore such summons because the failed auction left us feeling very vulnerable.

'So what do you want me to do?' asked the opposing senior counsel Deepak Nagpal (name changed), once we reached his plush office.

We were taken aback by this blunt yet loaded question. Thankfully we had come to the meeting together, even though Dhimant wasn't originally supposed to be there.

We were on the same page: there's nothing to say, let's meet in court. Either of us, if alone, may have even stated this out loud, but we realised it would be poor strategy to let our gloves come off here. We also realised that this message was not meant for us. Deepak Nagpal expected us to relay this message to Mr Shetty. We absorbed the message, did not react negatively, and left soon without saying anything. We never reverted to the senior counsel, nor relayed any message to Imtiaz, who had acted as the messenger. We never discussed this meeting with anyone and maybe it is destined for even Mr Shetty to read it for the first time in this book!

A few weeks later, Dhimant was waiting in the crowded passageway of the NCLT courtroom in Cuffe Parade to be called in for the hearing when Adv. Deepak Nagpal walked in. We were not expecting him to come in for this hearing because usually the opposing side did not send senior counsels for 'routine' hearings. We were among the few people who fielded our senior counsel on most hearings. 'He might have come for some other case,' Dhimant thought, but all his internal alarm bells were ringing loudly. He had come to the court to argue on this routine hearing to show us how he could cause havoc in our lives because we had not taken the rope he gave us. He had come to pull the rope tight.

'Hello I'm Dhimant Bakshi, from Imagicaa. We met some time ago,' Dhimant said, walking up to him.

Deepak looked him over as if he didn't recognise him. This would happen often, as people would remember Mayuresh rather than him, and Dhimant was quite happy to be under the cover of that invisibility cloak—it allowed him to observe the differences between what people said and how they reacted. Coming from a retail background, he would notice the brands and styles the people we met wore, and sometimes these gave him clues about the person behind the table, like a Mont Blanc cufflink worn by a mid-level young official of a company raised questions about how he could afford it. Sometimes these clues spoke louder than the person. Deepak drove a gold-coloured BMW. There were no subtle hints about him.

As Deepak walked towards the courtroom, Dhimant quickly rushed through the crowds milling around the courtroom to find Prateek. He just about explained the details of our meeting with Deepak and his fears regarding his sudden appearance before our matter was called out.

He wasn't wrong. Deepak had come to prove a point. But no matter how hard he tried, Prateek Seksaria was stamped all over that day! We watched the session unfold dramatically. Deepak left no stone unturned to make his point for admitting Imagicaa into NCLT right then and there. Prateek argued each point with logic, acumen and measured aggression and struck hard when the moment was right. Prateek carried that day on his capable shoulders. His sheer ability to dominate over Deepak, his instinctive knowledge of when to tone down and when to interrupt or raise objections and his absolute command over the process were enthralling to witness.

It was such a mesmerising session that when it ended, we felt like getting up and cheering like the cheerleaders one would have seen in the movie *Jolly LLB*. Prateek's spirited defence, high-voltage oratory and his absolute spirit to put in his all for us got us a much-needed breathing time. It also sent a strong message to Deepak Nagpal, and he never tried his luck with us again.

This encounter again taught us that we cannot afford to take any hearing lightly, especially in such matters. We needed a senior counsel with us for most of the hearings and no cost was too high for that, considering the value we gained.

## Documentary Trail

By February 2020, we had been battling NCLT admission in court for one-and-a-half years. NCLT proceedings are not supposed to last longer than six months so, understandably, it was getting a little difficult for the lawyers to continue defending us. The court's view was that this had gone on for too long. The NCLT bench had said on one occasion that 'we have to admit your matter and cannot delay it further'.

Prateek would often tell us, 'Everything is just a story in thin air, till you have the documents to prove its truth.' We needed documentary evidence to prove that: a) we were in talks with potential investor, b) investors were in talks with the lenders to make a proposal or an offer and c) banking officials were considering the proposal submitted. Most times, we had verbal updates about the transaction with that investor, which wouldn't suffice. 'Judges will never accept these "stories" if there is no written proof,' he would reiterate.

We were actively looking for more investors since this whole process of NPA and NCLT started and had had the foresight to keep all the banks informed. Every time we met a potential investor who looked credit-worthy, we would sound off our banks. We also made a written offer to the entire lender consortium for a one-time settlement (more on this in Chapter 5) and paid a token amount of ₹6 crore to the lead bank. After doing this, we informed the courts that we were settling with all our lenders and filed an affidavit pleading with them to grant us time.

However, convincing bankers to provide anything in writing was another uphill task. Bankers avoid settlement related correspondence like a cat avoids water, and no one wants to put their name on anything. This is understandable. There are even very competent bankers whose hands are very often tied down from fear of adversity, and that sometimes delays and even derails the process. However, we still couldn't get any documentary evidence from them, even though we had rebuilt some of the burnt bridges with the bankers after the failed auction. Fortunately, in February, we got an affidavit from the lead bank dated 17 February 2020 supporting our statement that Imagicaa was in talks for settlement and they had received the proposal, which was approved by the bank management to proceed, on a Swiss Challenge (a kind of a bank auction; more on this in Chapter 8). With this document, we felt on relatively safer ground at the next hearing.

But on 3 March, the same bank shockingly filed another affidavit with NCLT stating that they were withdrawing their previous affidavit because the company failed to convince the other lenders in time. It was a complete U-turn from their earlier position and put us in a fix. The timing of the statement was astounding as well, since there were barely seven working days from the date of the previous affidavit and approval from the lead bank, which was too little time for any other lender to move, leave alone get approvals from respective committees. We realised there was more to it than met the eye.

Our next court date was on 4 March 2020, just *one day* away. If the new affidavit was accepted, it would offer strong grounds to the bench to admit Imagicaa into the NCLT court, and that would mean the end of our innings. Insolvency proceedings would begin.

Despite all frantic efforts to meet the chairman of one of the banks after the second affidavit, we were refused appointments. Highly demotivated, expecting the worst but still hoping for a miracle, the two of us attended the court meeting thinking that we were nearing the end of this battle, one we would lose. The body language of our lawyer seemed defeated, since this affidavit had come out of the blue and we had little time to devise a fresh strategy. As a stopgap measure, we had prepared another affidavit for the court, which said that there was some confusion because the two bank affidavits contradicted each other, so we were requesting for some time to clarify the bank's position. That was the only strategy we could go with on that day. It all depended on the judge, and we prayed for a lenient view.

The court was packed as usual. Dhimant and the lawyers were in the crowded court room, while Mayuresh waited in the congested passage. Our junior lawyer had just messaged on our WhatsApp group that the matter would start in 5 minutes. Suddenly a very senior banker, Rajnish Sarathy, from the other lender bank who had also filed for NCLT proceedings against us, strode in, purpose written in every step and panting a little in the early summer heat. Mayuresh instinctively realised that he came with no good intentions towards us, as senior bankers usually do not appear for hearings. There was a merger taking place among the PSU banks and from thirteen, the number came down to ten by the time of the resolution. The application was filed by the bank that merged with the larger bank, such that the application now came from the larger bank.

Without thinking, Mayuresh quickly walked up and stood in front of Rajnish. He was a little startled but stopped out of courtesy. Mayuresh then asked him how he was doing and what brought him here on this very hot day. Searching for more things to ask, he said, 'How is your merger going?' He also told him our case was delayed and would likely come up after fifteen or twenty minutes.

Initially, Rajnish was in a rush while answering, then possibly seeing Mayuresh outside the courtroom too, he must have thought that the matter was actually delayed. After a couple of minutes, however, he assertively stated that he must enter the courtroom now and strode on like he had a mission to achieve.

Meanwhile in the courtroom, Dhimant briefed Prateek, who thought on his feet. He saw an opportunity for a mention and made his argument to the judge about the confusion in the affidavits. After hearing both sides, the judge granted an extension of one month. Rajnish entered the courtroom just as the judge finished dictating the order to the court reporter, announced the extension and moved on to the next matter. Rajnish turned red in anger and told his lawyer that he had got management directives to get the matter admitted in this session. He added that he had come with the sole aim of telling the courts that the second affidavit was the stated position of the bank. His lawyer scoffed and said, 'It's important for you to be here in time. If you had shared this update clearly, I could have pressed it.'

But the court's decision had already been made!

## An Amigo by Your Side

That day, 4 March 2020, we were truly saved because Imagicaa had been in the NCLT courts far longer than most cases, and Rajnish's view, along with the mandate from the bank, would have definitely led the judge to rule against us, and we would have lost our ongoing battle. It would not only have partially destroyed or at least disrupted the business, but also led to a significant value destruction for the lenders. It would have eroded the brand perception in the mind of consumers and employee morale would have simply come crashing down. The rollercoasters and magical rides would have possibly been dismantled and sold for scrap or at salvage value, as at that time there were no buyers of the company at the prices sought by the lenders. Maybe within a few years, you would find some real estate project on the site, and no remnant of the wondrous time millions of people had 'flying' over India, screaming through the loops of Nitro or their joyful shrieks at the wave pool. Thoughts of such a future chilled us to the bone.

Going back to the real question which stumped us that day, 'Why on earth did the bank suddenly want to withdraw the affidavit?'

Over many months, we pieced together the puzzle. Banks have a stringent hierarchy system and, at that time, there were two different mergers among five of our lender banks. Bank mergers are complicated affairs—you never know who is going to supersede, who is going to be the boss and what the organisation structure will look like. There is a lot more flux within the teams, and suddenly decision making takes a backseat. At that critical point, a smaller bank that viewed us negatively merged with a bigger bank that supportive of us. Later, we were given to understand that was the negative opinions coloured the other bank's views and possibly pushed the tide towards NCLT as a resolution tool.

It was an unpredictable time, and our teamwork, coupled with an unconventional and sometimes even wacky approach, saved the day!

Due to Mayuresh's quick thinking, we got a reprieve for a month, but that month turned into two years because COVID-19 reared its ugly head in the second week of March 2020, and the whole world got shut down. When the courts reopened after the lockdown, they addressed only emergency cases, that too online. Ours didn't count as an emergency.

COVID-19 drastically changed every equation that we and the banks had drawn up in our minds. The banks saw a drop in our value because Imagicaa was shut down due to the pandemic, and any prospective buyers would either get further disinterested or would quote a very low number. Thus, they became more amenable to waiting and watching and focused on dousing larger fires in their portfolio.

At this point of time, we picked up our earlier conversations with the Malpani Group, since we always believed they would be the most appropriate strategic promoters due to their experience in amusement parks coupled with utmost humility, long-term approach and strong belief in this category.

*Amigo Mantra #11:* Jab hogi ladai tab kharid lenge bandook, jab hogi ladai khatam to bech denge bandook. *When there is a battle situation, we'll buy a gun. When the battle ends, we'll sell the gun. Overhanging worries can be parked aside so we can focus on the present situation with rigour.*

*Amigo Mantra #12:* Aaj nikal gaya, kal ki kal dekhenge. *Today has gone. We'll see about tomorrow when it comes.*

# Thought #4: Legal Linguistics

*Hard learnings in the hallowed halls*

For NCLT cases, lawyers start by asking, 'How much time do you need to arrange funds?'

Our intention was to find a buyer or investor, and we needed some time for that. When we started, we thought six months would suffice to find a buyer or investor. In most cases, NCLT courts don't last longer than a year.

NCLT cases are not treated with top urgency by defending lawyers, possibly due to the nature and process of the Insolvency and Bankruptcy Code (IBC), 2016. Usually, law firms wait for a few months before assigning a senior counsel and let the junior lawyers handle the initial sessions. Here, they look for technical defects or maintainabilities in the cases before getting into the merit of case. Maintainabilities are grounds wherein the case does not get listed at all, such as questioning the jurisdiction, limitation period (cases barred by time), etc. This attitude percolates down to owners of the companies under litigation, because everyone thinks that the first few sessions are not important. However, if we had been fined a penalty or the judge had put in an unfavourable remark, the case would have begun with a black mark against us. That's why whenever we meet people who are going through the NCLT process, we always advise them to treat each hearing with equal gravity, because you never know when you may lose the direction of the case despite having the genuine intention of reviving the company. At such a juncture, when your company is going through NCLT, the goal should be to take the company out of the legal woods and focus on turning around the business. Through it all, the least you can do is to avoid any remark or a penalty from the court that might negatively affect your case somewhere down the line.

## The Cost of It All

While choosing a senior counsel, we were asked if we wanted the best or wanted to negotiate down the price, which would mean choosing one with less experience. We realised that this important decision was in fact a no-brainer if we wanted to get past NCLT. A good lawyer can define the trajectory of a case, and although we were cash-strapped and this was clearly a non-budgeted spend, we chose to go with the best.

This decision is repeated many times along such a journey, because before every hearing, law firms ask you if you think you need a senior counsel to appear (since most stressed companies may genuinely be unable to honour the bill).

The fact is that if any company lands in the NCLT court, no matter how genuine their intent is in paying their lenders, they still need to prove that they are eligible for a second chance and why that chance should be outside the bankruptcy courts. That's a huge point to prove and has many variables. An experienced senior counsel is your biggest insurance against a bad day at court.

## Bundling or Not

A few months after RTPL, another lender also filed an NCLT case against us. Now we had two cases and a choice to make—should we bundle the two cases into one?

After a lot of thought, we finally decided not to club the two cases as a strategy because it's a basic rule of war that you don't want your opponents to be united against you. Sometimes one opponent is more reasonable than the other, and you will lose the benefit of that situation if they fight together.

This situation doesn't follow the rules of maths where two negatives make a positive; here two negatives can make a bigger negative. Also, as we saw in the case where the views of a smaller lender bank coloured the view of a bigger bank because of a merger, a tail can very well wag the dog.

Of course, it was more expensive to tackle the two cases independently. In fact, at times, we had an overdue status with the law firms and had to spend time explaining our situation to them. We even got a dressing-down from them, but it all turned out well in the end. Many lawyers only work with an advance on such cases, but we were lucky to get some very supportive people on our side.

We chuckled to ourselves at times, 'Hope our own lawyers don't drag us to NCLT for their unpaid dues!'

## The Courtroom

The NCLT court in Mumbai took some getting used to. It was housed in the former MTNL building located near the Flora Fountain. The building was not created as an imposing courthouse and, unsurprisingly, was always packed, right from the courtroom to the passages. You never walked easily into the courtroom but elbowed your way through a sea of black capes.

On one occasion in the monsoons, Mayuresh jocularly visualised both of us walking and elbowing our way through this like Sunny Deol strode through a sea of black umbrellas in the Bollywood movie *Arjun*!

The NCLT court was very different from the way most of us envision courts with a witness box, public zone and the lawyers' bench standing at a respectful distance with ample space for the lawyer to stride around and make a point. On our first day in the court, as we jostled our way towards the courtroom, we noticed a pile of laptop bags in the passage. We were told that lawyers and clients deposit their paraphernalia of bags and briefcases in the narrow passage because there is no space in the courtroom. Later, as we became more conversant with the ways of the NCLT courts, we too would add our laptop bags to the ever-increasing pile in the passage.

The reason for such a congested court building was that the IBC was still a relatively new act in 2019 (it was notified in the *Gazette of India* on 28 May 2016). New courts had to be quickly created for it. Plus, there was always a whole line of cases waiting to be heard, because no one was clear about the exact time they would be called for. People were simply informed about their appointed day, which didn't allow for a staggering of the crowd.

## Maintainability

Initially, we used to think that in court the matter is always argued. That's what we see in the movies. But reality is quite different. The first few sessions went by without any argument or hearing. Only new dates were given—*tareek pe tareek.* Our lawyers would tell us, 'Now they will have to file a rejoinder, or a fresh affidavit' or 'Now this is not maintainable'. We didn't know what to make of it and would get worried about the actual outcome of our visits and the case itself.

It took us some time to understand the mechanics, and we learnt that lawyers use maintainability to gain time for resolution. The first question of 'how much time do you need?' gives lawyers an idea of how long they need to plan for maintainability. Lawyers try to poke holes into the NCLT submission on technical grounds. Discrepancies like an out-dated board resolution added to the submission, a document in the name of a senior manager signed by a junior manager, missing annexures like the initial sanction letter or loan agreement document—these make the judge set another date for the hearing so that the opposing party can 'cure the deficiency and refile it'. They usually look at all the documents with an eagle eye if the client wants an extension. If the client is ready with a resolution, then lawyers might not look at all these details.

This tendency of the courts to give *tareek pe tareek* came to our rescue in darkest hours. Time was our real ally!

## Attending ALL Hearings

Our lawyers often told us that we were the only clients who didn't expect the lawyers to just wave a magic wand and win the case for them. Neither of us *ever* missed a hearing and that stood out in all our legal trysts. We never took any hearing casually and would leave all other important tasks of the day to attend them. We knew that a lot of time was lost in travelling and waiting to be called, but we also knew the utmost importance of the twenty or thirty minutes that we got to listen as our lawyer presented our case in front of the judge. While showing up for each and every hearing, we created a sense of continuity. The lawyers and the teams knew that we were serious about the issue and, more importantly, we managed to get some or the other document at the right time and were right there backing our lawyers at every step with it.

We attended all preparatory meetings too. Many do not realise that preparatory meetings are important as top lawyers handle multiple cases. Like it or not, you are another 'case' for them—so the preparatory meetings serve to refresh their memory, broach key merits and share any updates that could prove precious in the courtroom the next day.

A big learning for us was that communication and sometimes even over-communication with lawyers is paramount. You need to repeat every small detail because it can help them defend you better. Mayuresh is a master archiver. He always has a copy of every single document, from an implied assent that we might have received from banks to minutes of meetings and other such details. His eyes would light up when lawyers probed us for such cues. These documents were a gold mine for the lawyers, as they could show the required evidence in court.

Often during an argument in court, the lawyer would make a point and would need evidence to prove it. While his juniors looked for the document or the date (it would take time because they are preparing for multiple cases) Mayuresh would provide the details or even a photocopy of the document to present to the bench. The fact is, every case gets a limited time for a hearing and you have to make the most of it. And because we were there, we were able to intervene when it mattered.

# 5

# Living in Complicated Times

*'Don't worry, I know that this investor has much more than the required funds.'*

ONE DAY IN FEBRUARY 2019, WHEN WE WERE JUST OVER SEVEN months in our NPA journey, the two of us found ourselves in the small, tight bylanes of Kurla, in the fringes of the almost-slums neighbouring Mumbai's tony Bandra–Kurla Complex.

We were looking for a 'solid' investor. But we were completely perplexed and almost lost.

The two brokers, Vishnu and Rao, who had got us to this 'pucca-your-work-will-be-done-here' meeting place looked befuddled and uneasy in these surroundings.

'You said you knew these guys would deliver on our requirement … don't you know them? Haven't you been here earlier?' asked Dhimant.

As soon as these words were out of his mouth, we realised it was too late in the day to be asking this basic question. This was the first time we were trying to meet investors who were not white-collar professionals, and we were completely at sea in this new landscape of individual investors.

## 1% Hope

The 1% Hope principle inspired us to continue till we crossed this phase. It was a philosophy that became our guiding light for many decisions as we looked for an investor or a buyer. There was no right or wrong here, no prejudices—we just kept moving ahead on hope. We took to it because this philosophy reminded us of what the character of Andy Dufresne says in one of our favourite movies, *The Shawshank Redemption*: 'Hope is a good thing, maybe the best of things, and no good thing ever dies.'

Hope was all we had, and being hopeful was what we decided to be. Our choices make what we are at the end of the day. This is how we got into never-give-up mode!

With these thoughts in mind, we had started widening our sphere of investors. In fact, we got another nudge in this direction when we started receiving forwards on WhatsApp from acquaintances about Imagicaa. People (brokers or wannabe investment bankers) we didn't know had created detailed documents on WhatsApp describing our company data, loan amount and potential settlement value. These documents were being sent without any restriction across WhatsApp. Some enterprising people even had the gall to put a footer with their name to show that it was their document. We were becoming famous for all the wrong reasons!

Since we were becoming famous, or infamous, we decided to listen to whoever turned up with a *solution* and give them a fair and patient hearing. It was interesting to see the perspectives people came with because they could go either way—some made us look at the same thing in an interesting new light, while some made us laugh out loud. Either way, it broke the monotony of the day. That's the simple reason of why we were lost in the bylanes of Kurla.

The reality was a little more complex.

Our so-called problem-solving brokers Vishnu and Rao were also apparently newbies to broking. One of them, Vishnu, was a former tabela (dairy cattle shed) owner! Vishnu's tabela had become a prime property during one of Mumbai's expansion periods, when the city loosened its belt to provide for overflowing demand. He had monetised his real estate for an astounding amount. Now that he had lots of money and ample time to spend, he had decided to become a broker and get more deals with his newly acquired skill. He and Rao had been vetted over a few rounds of discussion by Amarnath, a member of our accounts team. They had a fair idea of the amount we were looking for because Amarnath had repeatedly told them that we needed at least ₹700 crore to tide over the debt.

'Don't worry, I know that this investor has much more than the required funds,' Vishnu had said after eliminating other investors from his 'list'. Despite the assurances and the weeks of discussions with Amarnath, we were bemused when Vishnu said that this was also the first time he was meeting with this wealthy investor, the solution to all our problems!

## Through the Gates

Mayuresh had earlier gone with Rao and Vishnu to meet one of the gatekeepers of the investor, called Guru Rajput to check the investor himself first, before they met Dhimant.

As he entered the chosen conference room, a group of men stood up. Then the sea of men parted, and a giant of a man walked towards him, holding out his hand. His confident steps and arrogant walk were reminiscent of Spot Anna from the film *Pratibandh*.

Tall, muscular and bearded with long oily hair, this was Guru, the proposed investor. He was clad in a white kurta pyjama, and three thick golden chains dangled around his neck. A few gold bracelets and chains were on his wrists and multiple rings on his fingers. Guru was everything you would picture a Bollywood bhai to be.

Guru began the conversation by saying, 'I have a bungalow in Kharghar, but I have come all the way here because you are a good party.' Was this said to flatter Mayuresh or give himself an air of importance?

While talking to new investors, Mayuresh always looks for points that can help him tick them off as being credible. In Guru's case, he quickly said that the deal would be done through a very premier law firm in Mumbai because they were his 'seth's' lawyers. Hearing the name of this particular law firm gave his credentials a green tick—a reputed Parsi firm like this one would only have credible clients. Then Guru said that they could give much more than ₹700 crore. 'We can give around ₹1000 crore.' This again sounded like music to Mayuresh's ears.

After that successful meeting, Mayuresh also checked up on the company details of Guru's 'seth'. Quick research on ZaubaCorp about Guru's company showed a registered company with a car fleet business. All these tick marks—the premier lawyer, the reaction to ₹700 crore and the legitimate nature of the owner's company made us feel that we were possibly heading somewhere relevant and interesting.

A few days later, we were asked to assemble at a certain address in BKC. When we were halfway there, we received an updated address in Kurla East. It was a congested area and, as we had never quite been to that part of Mumbai, we relied on Google

Maps to take us there. At one point, it became evident that going ahead in a car would be impossible because the lanes were too narrow. We left our car behind and went ahead on foot. Turning another bend, we saw another alley of narrow crisscrossing lanes and that's when Mayuresh made a quick decision on a gut feeling—he quickly shared our location on Google Maps with an office colleague saying, 'Last seen at X'. We were definitely concerned for our safety, so this was a backup measure.

The two of us soon found ourselves walking through lanes that were no wider than the full stretch of our arms, with narrower pathways crisscrossing in between. Finally Google Maps informed us that we had reached our destination. Looking around, we found a huge compound with several cars parked on our right that opened to an old, dilapidated building with

peeling paint and rusted shutters. By this time, we were ready to imagine the worst because it seemed like we had just survived a Bollywood movie chase scene.

## The Set-Up

The interiors of the building contrasted starkly with the dilapidated exterior. Shiny marble floors with golden carpets, bright pink and green walls with large frames of holy places, elaborate china for serving water and a huge paan-daan completed this look of opulence. We were told to leave our shoes outside the door and then were taken into a smaller antechamber and asked to wait.

'*Seth kidhar hai?*' Mr Khan, our host, asked as soon as he walked in. He was wearing a white safari suit and was evidently expecting Mr Shetty. His question put us on the back foot. Mayuresh attempted to explain to him that we were CEO and the CFO and we had the authority to represent the company. In some time, Mayuresh was able to calm down Mr Khan by assuring him that the next time we would come with Mr Shetty.

'You are an NPA. We don't fund NPAs.'

This remark from Mr Khan again led Mayuresh to another long explanation about why we turned into an NPA. Mr Khan seemed to think we were wilful defaulters and initially looked affronted at the idea of funding an NPA, but after Mayuresh's spirited defence of our history and series of actions, he decided to deliver a sermon instead on his work ideals. Somewhere while mentioning grand philosophies of life, he mentioned Gautam Buddha's ideology and related it to his thinking. There was no stopping him after that, we heard him out in bemused silence as he told us how he was friends with all the big names, classmate of the chief minister then and how he had risen from poverty and made his own mark in the world. Wrapping up his long speech, he said that they had already made enquiries on the promoters and the project, and meeting the two of us had cleared some of his doubts. He felt that Imagicaa could be turned around, so he would consider funding the settlement.

We finally left that meeting with a list of bank and corporate documents that they required and an assurance that we would bring Mr Shetty on our next visit. To our utter bewilderment, after we narrated the discussions we had had with the newly found investors and described the location, Mr Shetty agreed to meet them.

Mr Shetty's visit became the highlight of Mr Khan's day. During the second visit, he posed for a picture with Mr Shetty and tried to show off his connections again by name-dropping some real estate developers and producers whom he assumed would know Mr Shetty. He tried to build a rapport by appreciating his grand vision to build Imagicaa and further mentioned that with his strong connection with the who's who of Mumbai, he would put Imagicaa on a high-growth trajectory. Nothing seemed impossible. After a few more general discussions, Mr Shetty came to the point and asked when both parties could sign the MoU to formalise the funding modalities, following which an agreement could be drafted to capture the details. On hearing this question, Mr Khan and Guru seemed stumped for a moment, then they quickly recovered. 'You will get the MoU in a few days. Just send us the documents we asked for,' they said.

This clever response put the ball back in our court. Neither of us was comfortable sharing these documents, as they had asked for the Aadhar cards of the directors as well as Imagicaa's GST returns and bank statements. As a listed company, there are many documents that we don't share freely. So for a few days, we decided to wait it out. Mr Shetty's simple diktat in many situations was, 'Don't do anything wrong.' If we only knew the context of what it meant in this particular situation!

A few more days went by, with us asking for the MoU and their counter-response asking for the documents. Finally, one of the brokers intervened and got the MoU from them. We quickly opened the document to check the details.

It was such a let-down!

The MoU was just a generic template and contained nothing specific about the terms, the lender or the value promised. Nothing, nothing at all!

They had left blanks in the places where more information was needed and had given it just to show that they had fulfilled their part of the bargain.

Again, the ball was in our court.

We spent a day preparing the file and deliberating on which sensitive documents to share. After this effort, we were still loath to handover the details, so we decided to go ourselves instead of sending a peon with the file. Guru and Khan again met us. After giving us another spiel on his unique thought process, world philosophies and ideologies, Mr Khan let Guru do the talking.

'Where is the 0.1%?' Guru asked.

We had no idea what he was talking about. There was never a discussion of any 0.1%.

'Didn't we tell you last time? It's the processing fees. Bhai, you need to give 0.1% processing fees for lawyers and their charges. That comes to ₹70,00,000 in cash. Anywhere you go the processing fees is 0.5% to 1%. We are charging a very low amount. At least arrange 7 lakhs immediately so that we can start work. The balance needs to be paid within one month. Only then we can share next steps.'

Mayuresh then started to explain to them that we were an NPA and had to take approval from the banks before making every single payment and a payment in cash was just out of the question. We could only do bank transfers. All this was true, but the underlying fact was that we still didn't have any conviction in this deal and we couldn't say that while we stood in their den.

To delve deeper, and to check on their claims, Mayuresh then asked about the premium lawyers they had referred to earlier, thinking that we might get some more information from the lawyers if we could get in touch with them.

But Guru completely backtracked with a plausible reason. 'We don't use them for smaller amounts, and plus you already have a time challenge on your hands with your banks. They will take a long time and you want it done fast. We'll use Mr Goyal, a high court advocate.'

Hearing this, Mayuresh again insisted that Guru ask this lawyer now because we didn't want to go back without any outcomes to relay to Mr Shetty. With the demand for processing fees and no premier lawyer, this meeting was not giving any great answers to our problem.

Finally, to answer some of Mayuresh's questions, Mr Khan took out his phone and spoke to his lawyer. 'Hello, Goyal saab, send the MoU and get the registration done.'

We left this meeting in a sombre mood because we knew there was no way we could participate in such a fashion, leave aside paying them 7 lakhs to begin with, that too in cash. As we were putting on our socks and shoes before leaving (it was customary to leave footwear outside before meeting Mr Khan), Mayuresh suddenly remarked, 'He didn't dial any number. He just unlocked the phone and spoke into it. Did you notice ... there was no wait time between the time Khan picked up his phone and spoke? He just spoke into a phone without dialling!'

We stared at each other, aghast.

A chilling suspicion began to form in our minds. Dhimant remembered that as we were walking into the small antechamber for the meeting, he had observed Mr Khan behind a half-opened door. It was a brief sideways glance, so he didn't make anything of it. Thinking back, he realised that the unreality of that moment had caught his attention. Mr Khan was dressed as usual in his spotless white safari suit and seemed to be asking someone else (who was hidden behind the door) if he was looking all right. That image stuck in Dhimant's mind because Mr Khan was always so confident and unassailable in front of us. He owned his look, but the way he was asking the person seemed completely out of character. He was behaving as if he was wearing a costume for a stage performance, something different from our normal attire.

Our doubts started growing. We decided to wait and see what happens. We didn't talk to them for a day, and that's when calls started coming. First Guru called, asking for cash, which we refused, repeating that as a listed company we could not pay in cash but could try to pay to their bank account. Then he called again, giving us Mr Khan's wife's bank account number as an option, since it was the last accounting month of the financial year (March) and so their company accounts would get 'disturbed' by the payment. He then justified the given account by informing us that Khan's wife was in any case a 49% partner in the company. We didn't respond.

For a few more weeks, Guru kept sending reminder messages asking for the 0.1% and then finally stopped.

This was our introduction to the world of scamsters, the fallout of going where there was 1% hope. We could not avoid this, but it was definitely a learning and made us tread more cautiously.

Later, thinking about it, we realised that these people were ready to invest ₹700 crore (and didn't even bat an eyelid at ₹1,000 crore) without ever seeing the property. They never once asked for a tour, whereas professional investors like fund houses always spent time looking at and assessing the property. At that time, we felt that it meant they had ready money to fund the deal, but after many such incidents, Dhimant jokingly coined a maxim, 'Money is never a constraint for the one who has none!' Whether you say one crore or a thousand crore, it means the same thing to them because once you give them the processing fees, they might say you don't look like a viable option or just stop taking your calls.

How many of us would go back to those crowded bylanes and ask for our money back if the deal didn't materialise?

We met many variations of this processing fees scam during our NPA journey. Every time it happened, we didn't succumb to the pressure because one of us always spotted when there was something wrong: *dal mein kuch kalaa, aur yahan toh puri dal hi thi kaali*. That's why we feel that it is necessary that such meetings be attended by more than one person.

## The Never-Ending Discussion

Guruji walked into our office in October 2019. He was a saffron-clad priest from Andhra Pradesh who used to shuttle between different states of South India. He was introduced to us because he claimed to have connections with some of the largest trusts of India, which had large cash and gold reserves. When Guruji came into our lives, we were desperately looking for solutions in whatever form possible, so his monk robes and tika didn't unsettle us as much as they did our office colleagues and the park team, who believed that bereft of realistic solutions, we were now seeking divine interventions.

'*Sathiya gaye hai yeh dono*,' Mayuresh heard a comment in our office when we just exited one of the discussions with Guruji—these two have lost their minds.

Unlike others, Guruji insisted on visiting the park, the place of business that required funding, to evaluate it in detail. He was very impressed with the project and started to discuss possibilities, which he called the 'programme'. The park team were still not able to understand this investor's profile, especially Colonel Kale, Shivajee and Sitanshu, who would voice their concerns and opinions in their own unique style: Colonel was fatherly, loaded with British sarcasm and with grandiloquence, whereas Shivajee's non-verbal communication, through his expressions, was much stronger. Sitanshu had a young collegiate demeanour and would try to understand our thought process by quizzing us thoroughly.

This time we received a call late at night from Shivajee, who had never called for any such matter. He said, 'You really think this can work?' Immediately after Guruji had left after his visit to the park, he asked pointedly, '*Yeh kya ho raha hai, aap ko sahi mein lagta hai ki yahan se funding aayega*?' ('You really think any funding will come this source?')

Despite their scepticism, the hospitality teams never compromised on their treatment of guests and visitors, regardless of their perception and approach. There was never ever an instance where our standards dropped even a notch, and we gave the guests a complete walk-through of the park and explained the concepts in detail so that each one went back with a clear understanding of the situation and a positive impression. That was always one of the best compliments we received from almost every potential investor.

Guruji would come in like a whirlwind. Before his arrival, an entourage of brokers would arrive, telling us that he was in the area and would soon deign to visit us. Despite the entourage, Guruji was quite soft-spoken and, after the initial greetings, would start the conversation by saying, 'Saar, I have made a *programme* for you.'

Despite his religious leanings, Guruji had a very business-minded approach to funding and wanted to create a programme to get us funding. He had visited Imagicaa and he loved the property, thus his idea was to increase footfalls by creating targeted campaigns for his networks in South India. Guruji planned a well-coordinated system of bus operators and travel agents who would ferry people from the different states of South India to Imagicaa and back. He felt such programmes would increase the capacity utilisation manifold.

'Give me paper and pen,' he would say as soon as he sat down. Mayuresh would dutifully get him a few A4 sheets, and he would start ideating after drawing a swastika on the top.

We had around eight to nine meetings in a space of two or three months. Initially, we were interested, as some of his ideas sounded potent, but after some time we started losing patience because he would come at any odd time and then sit for hours scribbling on sheets of paper. Mayuresh was even ready to shut the door on this option as we were running out of time with the banks, so Dhimant offered to go instead and talk to Guruji.

We were ready to talk to anyone to look for a solution. At that time, we were also trying out another solution—a direct company offered one-time-settlement (OTS) to the banks. To drive this methodically and tick all boxes of a Prudential Framework and the legal and banking systems, we roped in Ashutosh Maheshvari as an investment banker. He not only helped us navigate the complexities of OTS but became a trusted advisor to whom we turned for many negotiations and structuring advice at various stages in our journey. His ability to dissect a complex problem with his razor-sharp mind was second to none. His idea was unique—he didn't take on vanilla assignments, but only the ones that were complicated and had scope for innovation. The OTS was heading towards a sum of parts transaction where Mr Shetty would effectively cede control, so it needed to be navigated properly to ensure a win-win scenario for everyone. With his binary approach and sharp responses, he was able to handle any question thrown at him. We would never hesitate to call him or his team at any time and take his advice and inputs before meetings with lenders and potential white-collar investors.

For this OTS, we had to again break down the business into core and non-core parts. Essentially, we divided it into three parts—park, hotel and land. The idea was to sell the different assets to different buyers under a resolution package with a change-of-management scheme. This would be following guidelines established by the RBI. This was not an easy task, because Imagicaa had been created with land, hotel and park assets all together, and dividing them up physically required a lot of planning. Looking at the paucity of investors and time, this looked like the only way to get out of NCLT proceedings and pay our lenders, because post the asset sales, we thought we would get an amount of ₹575 crore to pay the banks. In order to show the validity of this plan to the banks, we also needed to put an initial amount (earnest money) into the bank's escrow account to commence the process. As we were looking for options to fund the escrow account, we thought it could be a good test of Guruji's intentions and capacity to participate.

In one of the meetings, we politely asked Guruji to start the business association by paying ₹6 crore as token money against our hotel inventory as a security and gave him an MoU for that amount. We expected that since he had spent so much time reviewing the property and speaking with us, he might have spoken to his investor/s, but he barely looked at the MoU as he put it in his bag and barely referred to it throughout the conversation. His attitude and body language did nothing to reassure us.

We never really understood what the actual intent in his case was. He never acted like a scammer, and he did spend a lot of time ideating and creating business plans, but there was no concrete outcome. Often after his visit, we felt like we had just gone through a carousel ride in Imagicaa where, after covering a lot of distance, you are still at the same place or in a situation of 'circular reference' in Microsoft Excel. There was no solution in sight, only a repeat of the last visit. After we shared the MoU draft, his visits slowly reduced and slowly dwindled to nothing.

## The Games Ego Plays

After Guruji's exit, we still kept trying for a one-time settlement. The case was ongoing in NCLT courts, and we were conscious of the ticking clock. We had been fighting our case for more than a year and were getting desperate for a solution.

In the first quarter of 2020, we heard about a big-time doctor near the park who was interested in investing in Imagicaa. The information came through an acquaintance of Mr Shetty's, who knew some brokers and was connecting us with them. The acquaintance had no idea about the doctor. In fact, this whole episode of looking for and finally meeting this elusive 'doctor' made us understand this extremely complicated and connected web of brokers, where no one knows anyone, but everyone wants their respective commission.

Finally, after some vague talks, a meeting was organised where two to three people came and around four or five people joined on a con-call. The first meeting was all about putting names and faces together. No one at the meeting knew the doctor. They were all brokers who had never met him. Mayuresh now started the lengthy and frustrating process of unravelling who was who. Mayuresh has endless patience and an ability to be completely attentive and involved in such long, vague discussions in order to finally get one piece of valid information. He began by making it clear to the 'front facers' that the sooner they got us directly connected to the main person, the better chance we had to convert this deal to a reality.

It took a few weeks to piece together the different players in this deal. For brevity's sake, we have distilled our findings below:

- The acquaintance told Mayuresh that he came to know about the investor through a person named Ravi.
- Ravi said he did know of a doctor in Khopoli who was not the 'big investor', but that the doctor knew a bit more about the investor.
- Mayuresh then contacted the doctor (who we later came to know held a large parcel of land in Khopoli but had no investible surplus of reckoning) and was directed towards one Kulkarni, who was purported to be an investment banker. But after some discussions, Mayuresh found out that Kulkarni was not a full-fledged investment banker but an employee in a company. Due to his corporate job, Kulkarni was the first person in this chain who at least understood how corporates function. After some calls, Kulkarni said he didn't know the exact details as sought by Mayuresh and pointed us towards one Limaye.
- Limaye was the fifth person in the chain. He was a chartered accountant, and Mayuresh sensed he was asking relevant questions. After a couple of calls, he candidly admitted that he didn't know himself of the end source, but a real estate broker called Panse knew the investor personally!

Finally, Mayuresh felt we were reaching the end of the line. While he was still unravelling this convoluted chain, the brokers at the beginning of the chain started fearing for their commissions since they felt they had showed us their cards. We had to reassure them that they would be paid if the investment was successful.

Often when Mayuresh relayed these long conversations with brokers who only wanted their commission, without adequate knowledge or information of the matter at hand, it felt like we were in the parable of the blind men and the elephant. Each broker had their own focus and theory, no one knew nor cared if the investor fit our needs or if we fit the investor's requirements.

Mayuresh thought Panse would connect us to the investor, but talking to Panse was not easy. Panse had a huge ego that was easily pricked. He portrayed himself as a big operator, but over few calls, Mayuresh soon discovered that he was a small-time real estate agent in Pune. He would often cut his calls to show that he was too busy to talk. After a lot of cajoling and requesting, Panse finally gave the name of a business group and said Dr Venkat would invest. After a lot of persuasion, he 'revealed' that Dr Venkat was an MP in Telangana and represented a group of companies and he would soon come to meet us as this investment had come on his radar. Panse also cautioned us that we needed to refer to the gentleman as 'Dr Venkat' without fail. He had also added that Dr Venkat was a colonel too.

We finally had the investor's name. We promptly went on the net to check the details of the group. The basic website merely revealed that it was a diversified group with projects in petrochemicals, and we found one name in the list of directors list that could possibly be our Dr Venkat.

'Maybe that's him?' we thought.

Mayuresh even went through the entire list of 543 MPs to find more details, but that was a dead end there was no Dr Venkat there.

A few days later, we received a new message from Panse: 'You now need to sign a document stating that you are agreeable to hand over the company to Dr Venkat. Only after you sign that document will he talk to you or meet you.'

These terms were completely impractical for us. They might work for a private limited company, but we are a listed company and can take no major decision without informing the board of directors and taking their approval, along with informing the stock exchanges. Months of work seemed to be wasted by this untenable demand, yet working with our 1% hope ideal, we still kept looking for a way. After a few more weeks of Zoom and WhatsApp calls (those were the COVID-19 lockdown days) with Mr Shetty and company secretaries, we found a way where Mr Shetty would sign subject to the approval of the board, lenders and shareholders with additional conditions.

One of our key worries was that while we were doing all this to keep Imagicaa in working condition, we didn't have any idea about the new management or their plans for Imagicaa, so we now mustered the courage and asked, 'Once you acquire control, how do you plan to actually manage the company given your other pre-occupations, because Imagicaa has a unique business model?'

We thought that we would now find some solutions and start talking with Dr Venkat. But very soon we realised that it was beneath him to talk to us directly. He saw Mayuresh and Dhimant as employees of the company that he was soon going to own and nothing more. Dr Venkat's way was to send messages through Panse. The problem was that Panse had absolutely no idea of corporate requirements nor of the scale of the work at Imagicaa. He just repeated what he was told: 'You need to hand over all your control to us, we will take over all your liabilities and our turn-around expert will plan out the next steps.'

'Who is the expert? Have they ever run an amusement park of this scale?' we persisted, unabashed in our questioning.

After many such ping-pong discussions through Panse, we were given the name of the expert—Dr Bimal Das (name changed). Dr Das turned out to be a dignified Bengali gentleman of about seventy with vast senior corporate experience. He had a strong British accent and had a conventional but methodical approach. He understood our restrictions as a public limited company, but he also knew that Dr Venkat was open to only one way of working.

We had started looking for Dr Venkat in February 2020, and by the time we connected with Dr Das we were in the midst of the pandemic. India and the rest of the world were reeling under the first wave. The park was closed, and our hotel had been allowed to open at 50% capacity with several restrictions after a few months.

We planned our first meeting in a plush hotel in Mumbai keeping in mind the lockdown restrictions, but Dr Venkat insisted that he would meet us only at Imagicaa because he said, 'I already have a hotel in Imagicaa so why should I go to Mumbai?'

In his mind, he was already the whole and sole owner of Imagicaa. Despite all the egoistic talks and unreasonable demands, we could not walk away at that juncture because there was no other live option.

The details of the visit were as complicated as the man himself. He wanted a room whose number added up to nine. He further instructed us that he would go straight to his room on arrival and only come for the signing at a specific time to a specific room. Since most of the rooms were anyway vacant due to the COVID-19 lockdown, we could easily fulfil his demands, but there was a shortage of staff and the general manager would stare incredulously at us when we put these demands to him. To paraphrase Alice from *Alice in Wonderland*, 'It was getting curiouser and curiouser.'

Finally, after all these preparations, Dr Venkat arrived at Imagicaa on the designated day. We were surprised to learn that he had come in an Etios with terry upholstery. For all the egoistic bluster, we expected a luxury car at least, or some opulent interiors.

During the signing of the MoU, he again had very specific demands. The printer was to be kept in the meeting room. He also took offence at the way Mayuresh was sitting with his legs crossed in the meeting and said it was considered apshagun—inauspicious—in his village. It was a herculean task to get the MoU signed and focus on the content amidst all the astrological hocus pocus.

Finally, after the signings, we thought we would get more clarity on how he would settle or restructure the liabilities, but the only thing he wanted next was again far-fetched—to make him an executive director in the company. According to company rules, only a person directly involved with day-to-day operations can be considered for executive directorship, like the promoter, CEO or CFO. We said we could make him an additional director, but even though Dr Das understood where we were coming from, Dr Venkat refused any title lower than an executive director.

'We have more than thirty companies, and we can pass a board resolution anytime we want, that too in the manner acceptable to us,' was the terse message relayed through Panse.

Both of us tried to reason with him and explain that we were not a private limited company, but Dr Venkat was never ready to listen. In any case, we could only speak to him through Dr Das or Panse, not directly. The former understood how a company worked but could do nothing to help us, and the latter was absolutely out of his depth but refused to accept his shortcomings and try and understand the problem.

We often compared the acts of the so-called network of financial agents to the Bollywood movie *Malamaal Weekly*. Here, each one would think that they had found the solution without even knowing the problem, not having any acumen, and each one would be in the race to get to the elusive pot of gold. Exchanging business cards or mobile numbers was a complete no-no. It seemed like violating the unwritten code and bypassing the chain to reach to the end client.

This discussion had started with a chain of brokers, but after an arduous process had come down to three characters: Dr Venkat, Panse and Dr Das. Yet there clearly was a massive communication roadblock created by Dr Venkat, which prevented the deal from proceeding properly. We never got to discuss the required details and know the endgame for Dr Venkat. Neither did we find out who were the people backing him. It was quite frustrating, and finally, after lingering in the waters for some more time, the whole deal tapered out.

Incidentally, a few months later, a broker from Goa, who was apparently a hotelier too, mentioned how Dr Venkat was extremely difficult to work with. At least we were not the only ones to face this issue with him.

*Amigo Mantra #13:* Ulte ghade pe paani. *It's meaningless to drive sense into someone who does not get it!*

*Amigo Mantra #14:* Okhli mein sar, toh musalon se kya darna. *When you've already taken the risk, there's no point in fearing the consequences.*

## Thought #5: One-Time Settlement

Why were we looking for a one-time settlement by the end of 2019?

One of the key questions all the investors and financiers used to ask was, 'Your outstanding from the bank is ₹1,000 crore, and you are saying the banks might agree to a haircut and take ₹575 crore or ₹600 crore instead. But do you have any approval from the banks that they will agree to a settlement number?'

The fact is that no banker will ever categorically issue such a statement because stating that they are willing to take a haircut is a difficult exercise. The bankers have to go through an unbiased process of price discovery, then run it past their committees, which is fairly elaborate. It was more difficult in our case because there were thirteen lenders. To figure out the way ahead, we first went to the recovery department with a sum of the parts (SOTP) valuation to ask their views. Most of the senior officials said that they didn't want to know the details of how we were garnering the ₹575 crore—they just wanted one consolidated number. At this juncture, lenders missed that critical point of the promoter's preparedness to cede control and part with his dream in the interest of saving the company. It was a delicate and a very emotionally draining phase and despite us repeating it, it was never taken as a statement of fact. Perhaps the overhang of other NPAs and NCLT had a much larger impact on the lenders.

Arriving at a consolidated number for the bankers was easier said than done, because we had to sell different assets in parts, and it was unlikely to happen simultaneously. Further, we would need an NOC for each asset sale. Our earlier experience at getting an NOC from the banks for the sale of land before we turned NPA showed us that it could be a never-ending rigmarole—no banker would want to be the first to sign. It was completely understandable, because bankers would be questioned by their committees and would need detailed valuations. To formulate a feasible plan that would improve value and check all the process boxes, we created a package proposal for the recovery department team—₹575 crore, with ₹550 crore paid upfront and ₹25 crore worth of equity.

Even then, individual banks could not give us a letter saying they agreed on ₹575 crore. Since each bank had given us a different loan amount and collectively formed a consortium, they followed the sharing pattern on a pro-rata basis of the amount of loans advanced. The in-principle break-up of the settlement amount was noted in a bank consortium meeting where representatives of all the banks were present.

After this meeting, we realised that the minutes of a bank consortium meeting are a strong document and could be used in court because all the bank representatives sign it. There may be varying interpretations on some occasions, but when bankers agree that they are in principle fine with the ₹575 crore, subject to approval from their committees, then that becomes a starting point. Thus, minutes hold directional ramifications and can in a way facilitate decision making in the mammoth multi stakeholder banking system.

Another reason for finally getting a number crystallised was the litigation on some of the land parcels. The banks also understood that the litigant was obdurate and had already cost them a lot, i.e., the billionaire investor and funds alike. They saw how that could affect the marketability of the land. We think that his obduracy also led to a slight reduction of the bank expectations of ₹650 crore. Meanwhile, to prove our readiness for the one-time settlement, we deposited ₹6 crore with the banks.

That's how the number of ₹575 crore seemed settled in the system at that point of time.

A one-time settlement gave us three advantages:

- We could show potential investors that the banks would agree on a number closer to the realistic enterprise value.
- It kept the banking system engaged and showed them that we were serious and making headway in finding a solution.
- It created a record of formal correspondence with banks, which we could show in NCLT court as proof that we were working for resolution, giving us much needed breathing time.

# 6

# It's a NO Till You Ask

*'Yeh to sher ke muh se niwala nikalane ke barabar hai!'*

Since the NPA saga began, two things kept us going. One was that our business was operational and the second was that the senior team was around to ensure that our daily engine kept running and the asset remained in good condition. Now, while we were dealing with people like Dr Venkat and Guruji in 2020, Imagicaa Park shut down because of the pandemic. Our main source of income just stopped, and each passing day escalated to the damage to our business. We barely had any reserves to manage, as traditionally the March quarter was weaker than the others, and when the lockdown started in March 2020, we had wafer-thin balances in the bank account.

We were in a tight spot.

The lockdown continued for a very long time as entertainment was the last sector to be reopened. Shivajee, Sitanshu and Amit, alongside us, made significant efforts with governments, IAAPI and RAI to seek permission to reopen the park. From RAI, CEO Kumar Rajagopalan, Gautam Jain, Lawrence Fernandes and Akshay Kale, and from IAAPI, the members of the board as well as Anil Padwal were among the people who played a pivotal role in reopening parks after several meetings with officials and state leaders. Then starting January 2021, a miracle that we had worked very hard for finally came through. We received a total of ₹24 crore (in smaller tranches) as a GST refund.

Let's backtrack a bit.

In 2018, when Dhimant took over the mantle of the CEO, he heard whispers of a GST refund that was lawfully due to us. Imagicaa was constructed with the largest investment in the entertainment category in a C category Zone as per the Maharashtra Tourism Policy. Thus it was eligible for tax incentives from the Maharashtra government. When the GST rollout was carried out by the central government in July 2017, these incentives were not mentioned. Nobody knew what to do. Dhimant was sure that we could get the money back, but everyone else was sceptical. 'No one can get money out of the government,' they said.

How were we to ask the government for the money?

## Getting our Dues

We tried going to Mantralaya on several occasions and putting our case forward. Nothing moved despite multiple representations. Finally, we scheduled a meeting with an IAS officer, expecting that, being at a pivotal position, he would be able to guide us through the process. But he coldly told us that this was our business risk. His complete apathy made it sound like we were making personal profits from this situation. We did not know whom to connect with after this debacle and, running out of choices, we pushed the internal team to file a case against the government for a GST refund. Of course, everyone was not on board with this because they felt that we would jeopardise our relationship with the officials. Mr Shetty, however, strongly supported this step.

The difficulty was one thing. Others in the company couldn't see how it was all adding up and affecting our bottom line. Dhimant decided to make them see the impact of the money we were losing due to this payment. In every daily report, monthly business update and footfalls, he instructed the IT team to add a row showing the amount we were cumulating as SGST. This simple step showed the leadership how we were not availing income that was rightfully ours. It was an adaptation of 'What gets measured, gets done.'

Many people felt that highlighting an amount which we would never recover was a waste of time. Many a time, intellects and the self-proclaimed experts obstruct innovation or create a hostile environment, whereby making a seemingly futile attempt gets impossible. Thus, breaking this mindset was yet another important step. Dhimant was really inspired by Paddy Padmanabhan, Balagopal Vissa and Neil Bearden at INSEAD. Neil, who taught decision science, helped Dhimant form this mindset. This was alongside the book he recommended, *The Art of Thinking Clearly* by Rolf Dobelli. His alma mater INSEAD was key to giving him a unique perspective, and pearls in the INSEAD Brown Book added to his repertoire significantly.

When you are in a trough, you have everything to gain, so making an attempt is the real thing and not getting bogged down is key.

Our first lawyer was very learned and the founder of a highly reputed law firm, but he would just tell us the law and the process. After every meeting, we would return with our heads buzzing with facts but no way of going forward. It felt like playing brain teaser games, with no concrete output. We soon realised we needed someone to fight for us with an attitude to win. That's when Mayuresh pushed us to meet Vishal Kamat (MD of Kamat Hotels), who turned into our friend, philosopher and guide. His network, his wisdom and practical approach connected us to yet another star lawyer, Abhishek Rastogi. In him, we found a lawyer and a 1 a.m. call person who had strong instinct to win and make a mark for himself. An ambitious go-getter, he was super sharp with his ability to dissect a problem.

While we were fighting this in the court on one hand, the two of us started frequenting the Mantralaya to meet government officials with a much higher frequency. Very often, our teammates would call us bank and court employees. On many occasions, we would enter the office only after our court and bank visits when others were leaving after a regular day's work. It was almost like working a second or third shift. There were many instances where we would wait for hours before anyone deigned to speak to us, but this didn't bother us, because every meeting that materialised was a small step in the right direction for us. Another thing we learnt was to never say no to tea! It became one more reason to sit a bit longer with the officials and get more cues on handling the situation, explain matters in detail as well as understand the person better. Inefficiency in serving tea is what very often we would pray for!

Due to all these efforts, certain cabinet approvals came through in August 2019, barely a few weeks before the Assembly elections and the ensuing political drama in Maharashtra. A few weeks later, a new government was sworn in. Things slowed down as the new government settled in, to come to a standstill when the pandemic began. Fortunately, just on the verge of the nationwide lockdown, we had pushed for the release of a government resolution on 4 March 2020 pertaining to the cabinet approval of August 2019.

मुख्यमंत्री सचिवालय (जनसंपर्क कक्ष)

**मंत्रिमंडळ निर्णय**

**दिनांक : २८ ऑगस्ट २०१९**

**( बैठक क्र. २३५ )**

| अ.क्र. | विषय | विभागाचे नाव |
|---|---|---|
| १ | मुंबईतील उपकरप्राप्त इमारतींच्या पुनर्विकासासाठी मार्गदर्शक सूचना | गृहनिर्माण |
| २ | देशातील अभिनव प्रकल्प विकसित होणार नाशिकमध्ये मेट्रो प्रकल्प राबविण्यास मंजुरी | नगर विकास |
| ३ | ओल्या कचऱ्यापासून खत तयार करणाऱ्या शहरांना मिळणार प्रोत्साहन अनुदान | नगर विकास |
| ४ | सदनिकांचे अधिकार जमीन महसूल अभिलेखात नोंदविले जाणार | महसूल |
| ५ | अघोषित प्राथमिक, माध्यमिक व उच्च माध्यमिक शाळा व तुकड्या तसेच घोषित उच्च माध्यमिक शाळा व तुकड्यांना अनुदान मंजूर | शालेय शिक्षण |
| ६ | दारुबंदी अधिनियमात सुधारणा : गडचिरोली, चंद्रपूर व वर्धा जिल्ह्यांत गुन्हेगारांवर कडक कारवाई होणार | उत्पादन शुल्क |

पर्यटन धोरणांतर्गत पात्र पर्यटन प्रकल्पांना अनुज्ञेय वित्तीय प्रोत्साहनांच्या सवलतीपोटी वस्तु व सेवा करातील राज्याच्या हिश्श्याच्या रकमेइतकी रक्कम परतावा म्हणून अनुज्ञेय करणेबाबत.

महाराष्ट्र शासन

पर्यटन व सांस्कृतिक कार्य विभाग

शासन निर्णय क्रमांक : टिडीसी २०१७/९/प्र.क्र. १०४/पर्यटन

मंत्रालय, मुंबई ४०० ०३२

दिनांक : ०४ मार्च, २०२०.

वाचा:- १) शासन निर्णय क्र. एमटीसी ०३९९/प्र.क्र. १४२/पर्यटन, दि. ८ जुलै, १९९९.

२) शासन निर्णय क्र.एमटीसी २००५/प्र.क्र.१७२/पर्यटन, दि. १६ डिसेंबर, २००६.

३) शासन निर्णय क्र.टीडीएस २०१५/११/सीआर-१०२९/पर्यटन, दि. ४ मे, २०१६.

प्रस्तावना:

पर्यटन हे आर्थिक विकासाचे प्रमुख साधन म्हणून ओळखले जात आहे. अत्यंत कुशल ते अकुशल रोजगारांची मोठ्या प्रमाणावर निर्मिती करण्याची क्षमता पर्यटन व्यवसायामध्ये आहे. पर्यटनास वाव दिल्याने विदेशी मुद्रेच्या प्राप्ती समवेत पर्यटनयोग्य क्षेत्राच्या आर्थिक प्रगतीस वाव मिळणार आहे. वरील सर्व उद्दिष्टांचा विचार करुन महाराष्ट्र शासनाने उपरोक्त शासन निर्णयान्वये पर्यटन धोरण १९९९, पर्यटन धोरण २००६ व पर्यटन धोरण २०१६ जाहीर केले आहे. सदर शासन निर्णयांमध्ये ही योजना राबविण्यासाठी पात्रतेचे निकष, वित्तिय प्रोत्साहने तसेच कार्यान्वयन यंत्रणा स्पष्ट करण्यात आल्या आहेत. त्यानुसार पर्यटन धोरण २००६ व पर्यटन धोरण २०१६ अंतर्गत पात्र घटकांना प्राप्त होणारी वित्तिय प्रोत्साहने नमूद

*Extracts of State Cabinet Approval of August 2019 and thereafter Government Resolution (GR), which got finally issued on 4 March 2020, just before the COVID-19 lockdown hit the country.*

On a side note, 4 March 2020 was the date when another landmark incident occurred—the NCLT hearing where we almost got admitted into bankruptcy proceedings!

Through the pandemic, this refund became even more important for Imagicaa's survival, and we knew that we were close to getting a resolution, so we would go at least eight to ten times a month to plead our case and meet government officials. We knew that we couldn't let it go now. From April to September 2020, our innumerable visits led to the completion of all necessary applications, certifications and more needed for this refund. Finally, from January 2021, we started receiving the refunds.

Our efforts helped others too, because we were not the only beneficiaries of this step. But for us, it came at a time when we were going through a major financial distress and had reached the lowest in the company bank balance. This refund money came in tranches, and every time we received it, the first thing we did was to invest in the maintenance of the park and keep all our expensive rides in working condition. We also paid partial salaries to employees to keep their home fires burning. Then we paid our vendors and creditors who had supported us in the lowest period. That's one of the ways we survived the winter of COVID-19.

## The Good Ones

In this battle, we met some really amazing people too. For instance, Mayuresh would get in touch with a certain person he knew at the Mantralaya when we were just a few minutes away from the gate, and he would instruct the guard to let us in, which was a challenge due to COVID-19 restrictions! We didn't meet him till 2023, and he just knew us as some officials of Imagicaa. He always helped us in those vulnerable times, though he may have been busy at his high-pressure job too.

Another gem of a person was a senior government official in the Mantralaya. We would meet him for the GST case, and he would give us time and listen to us and understand the actual matter with logic. You have to start acting, and the rest will follow.

One providential day, both of us were at the court when the above-mentioned senior government official called Mayuresh late in the evening and asked him a question regarding the GST matter. As usual, Mayuresh thought on his feet and said that both of us would come over for an in-person clarification as we were 'just across the road' (in reality we were a good 25–30 minutes away). It turned out to be a pivotal moment for the case, and our dash to the Mantralaya was crucial, because the official was putting together a note capturing necessary information on our petition for a refund (to share with other departments) and we could clarify certain critical points to him.

He had more questions the next day, asking why we should be granted a refund since the tax was being collected from the guests. Mayuresh reasoned that this was not a general relief, but actually a government promise that had not been honoured. The purpose of the said relief/refund was to help partially recover the project capital expenditure. We stressed that at least the states' share be granted, which was 9% on the ticket sales. In fact, prior to the GST rollout, the said benefit was 15% on the ticket sales. Dhimant emphatically retorted, 'No private player will ever believe in government promises if such promises aren't honoured.' That sentiment was captured in the document the official prepared.

## Cut the Cutback

In 2020, another incident involved people saying 'they won't agree to this demand', but our obstinate refusal to stop asking yielded results. Ever since Imagicaa became an NPA in 2018, our lender banks imposed a 'cutback' on our accounts as we were unable to service the interest and principal of the loan agreement. What the cutback meant was that 5% of our revenue was retained by the banks through a 'hold on operations' mechanism. At regular intervals, the lead bank would disburse the collected amount into the respective lender accounts. This is a standard process for NPA companies, but no one foresaw the lockdown. Suddenly all textbook scenarios went out of the window. Imagicaa was completely shut down. The fourth quarter of the financial year is usually a low season, so we had sparse reserves and absence of flow of revenues meant that we didn't have enough money in the bank to pay our staff. It was a grim situation.

In a Zoom meeting with the senior management, we decided that we would disburse salaries on a sliding scale, with 70% of the frontline employees' salaries being paid, while mid-level and upper management would get 30% of their salaries. But we didn't have even that much in our bank account to honour this decision. Desperately looking for solutions, Dhimant realised we had ₹40–45 lakh lying in the primary bank's escrow account pending disbursal under 'cutbacks'. The bank had deducted the amount but had yet to distribute the money to the consortium members.

'Why can't the banks release this cutback to pay for park operations and our employees? We can recoup this immediately as we re-open or get our refunds,' Dhimant said, fully realising he was grasping at straws.

No one had ever thought of asking the banks or putting across a proposal of using the cutbacks. The first response from the team was, 'The banks will never agree. Remember, we are an NPA.'

Arvind said with his characteristic bluntness, 'It's never happened before. You don't understand the banking system. This isn't possible.'

We agreed. This was a valid response, but we were in the midst of a never-before-experienced time in recent human history. There was no playbook on what was possible and what wasn't. We had to deal with the current reality. Every day was a new lesson and a chapter that would be unique to us, so we had to deal with it with a fresh and open mind. We have no room to be complacent.

We decided to go ahead and explained the whole situation to our banker, making almost a mercy petition. He refused at first, then when we continued pleading with him, he listened attentively and genuinely understood our plight. He responded by saying, 'I will try. I cannot promise anything.'

That was enough for us. First step achieved!

The two of us crafted a proposal with key inputs from Arvind and sent it off with a prayer. In an inter-bank consortium meeting, the officials deliberated upon this request. There were murmurs and resistance from a few, but candid outreach from us, backed by a soft nudge from a couple of senior officials, led to the consortium finally approving the request. That's how we got about ₹45 lakh, which helped us survive the first lockdown. It was almost like oxygen to a person gasping for breath.

Bankers deal with many clients in a day looking for loans of ₹100–200 crore. Usually when you walk into the banks, you would be one more person with almost the same ask. You have to find a way to connect with the officials and build relationships.

Thanks to Mayuresh's experience dealing with bankers and the lending system since Imagicaa's inception, he thought he knew what a banker could do and what was beyond their purview. Dhimant had no such blinders, and he would go and directly ask why we couldn't do things a certain way instead of how it was traditionally done. Mayuresh would not stop him because he realised that even bankers found that way of looking at things refreshing. Dhimant's wit would make the situation very light, and we could both build a strong relation with the people we met. It often became the X factor that swung things in our favour.

Dhimant often behaves like a woodpecker. He keeps looking for a way to turn a firm 'no' into a 'yes'. He will send update mails, call to check on progress and keep looking for solutions, even when everyone has given up. There have been more than enough times when this 'woodpecker' attitude has got us unprecedented results!

*Amigo Mantra #15: Not to settle till you have an answer is the way to go.*

*Amigo Mantra #16: Never refuse tea, make the most of the time while the tea arrives!*

# Thought #6: *Ek se Bhale Do!* The Benefits of Going Together

Often people questioned us on why we went together for meetings with banks, lawyers, investors or even to address local issues. When both of us left the office, many discussions and signatures got delayed, since both of us were directly responsible for some of the key functions. Yet, after few of our encounters, we understood the importance of being together, especially in unpredictable situations.

'Warp and weft' is the phrase that comes to mind whenever we think of our partnership. Both of us have very different personalities, yet despite that—or maybe because of our different personalities and sometimes diametrical approach—we form a good team. Dhimant is assertive, funny and upfront, and he calls Mayuresh 'Swami dada' because he is the calmest man he knows and if Mayuresh ever gets angry with anyone, then you can be dead sure that the person completely deserved it!

Mayuresh grew up in a joint family with more than ten cousins and several uncles and aunts. Growing up like this, you learn to understand people better, and be more accommodating of individual needs and quirks. He spent a lot of his formative years in his ancestral house in Mumbai. Its doors were always open and numerous relatives, friends, neighbours would be in and out of the house through the day. Seeing so many people, views and ideas made him always ready to listen deeply and find amicable solutions.

Through this journey we met many people for different reasons, from asking for investments to updating lenders and pleading our case with government officials. There were many data points to collect and collate. For one person, this would be a lot to handle along with corporate responsibilities. Even for two it was a lot to handle, but we always knew that if one of us missed something, the other would catch it. Discussions with bankers, lawyers or investors could go either way, and we needed a person who would be on our side when things got ambiguous, delicate, rough or raucous—someone you could trust intuitively and whose opinion could strengthen your views. Each of us needed a friend, an amigo.

Both of us notice different things too, like in the case of KK, Dhimant noticed his demeanour while talking to a person behind a half-closed door, while Mayuresh noticed that they never actually spoke to anyone on the phone. Combining these two perspectives created a clearer and more comprehensive picture.

The best part was that in the middle of serious conversations, where we had no chance of exchanging notes on crucial questions, we would often not even need to look at each other to understand what our response should be, especially when we needed to respond independently to balance each other. We knew what the other wanted to say—the answer was in the slope of the shoulder, the measured movement of the hand or the tone of voice. Through all the ups and downs, the absolute menagerie of people we met and the various complications that arose, there was never an iota of friction between the two of us.

We often faced really tricky situations and we needed to make quick decisions, a simple yes or a no. These quick decisions had a high impact. Two people can take a more rounded and well-thought-out decision than one person who feels cornered.

One of us just had to say, 'we need to go for a meeting', and the other would get up and leave too. There were so many different people to meet, angles to try and work out that no day could be well-planned in advance; we worked like firefighters ready to move on a call. The best part was that neither of us ever had to explain to each other the importance of any visit. This strong understanding and trust between us helped us 'seize the day' and make the most of any situation. Our habit of usually going together made it easy for us to support each other instinctively through the various ups and downs and helped us avoid some situations like the one with Ajay Sharma, or when we were almost scammed by Guru and his team, which could have seen all our efforts wasted.

We don't disconnect. And one of the strongest bows in our quiver is our ability to laugh at ourselves and the situations we so often got in. It helped us relax and think empathetically. An incident comes to mind. A meeting was fixed with a highly recommended lawyer by the founder of our law firm, Ameet Naik of NNICO. He introduced us to a specialised advocate dealing in defamation matters. He is a dynamo himself, knew our pulse well and, with his network, he could determine who would be well-positioned to guide us well. The need arose because the obdurate litigant was creating a lot of trouble for us. Recently he had started personally targeting us through his proxy cronies. We wanted to file a defamation case against him. The lawyer advised us against filing a defamation case because 'in a defamation suit, you have to prove that you have some fame and at each step the opponent is going to throw one stone at you that will create ripples. You will have to ensure that you prove him wrong at each step!' Basically, he was saying that defamation cases are usually very tricky, and the onus of all providing proof of 'fame' lies on us, the plaintiffs.

Did we have that 'fame'?

It was quite a sobering thought that we would need to prove our so-called 'fame', that too in a situation when we ourselves were an NPA and referred to as 'defaulters'! We walked out of the consultation with his sombre words ringing in our heads, but by the time we reached the parking area, we were almost hysterical with laughter. Pedestrians on the road were staring at us.

We have laughed often at the improbable, unthinkable and bizarre situations life has turned our way, and that's been a great stress reliever.

*Amigo Mantra #17:* Kabhi khud pey, kabhi apne haalat pe rona aaya. *Sometimes, in the most difficult situations the best thing to do is to get on with it ... Just take a pause and a deep breath.*

*Amigo Mantra #18:* Nahi re... Kabhi khud pe, kabhi haalat pe hasna hai, par hasna zaroori hai! *Laughing, sometimes at situations and our own selves, turns out to be a simple and effective remedy to refresh and recharge.*

# 7

# Illusions or Delusions

*'Book my flight, you know I don't carry a credit card!'*

It was 24 December 2020, and we were running breathlessly through Kuala Lumpur International Airport to catch our flight back to Mumbai. We were horribly late.

We had left the hotel well before time, but our brokers hadn't. They tried to squeeze in a discussion on a separate deal of their own before flying out. To make matters worse, we hadn't factored in the terrible Christmas Eve traffic on the Jalan Subang highway. Desperate and stuck in the middle of the jammed highway, one of our brokers seriously considered asking for a ride on the tiny scooters that were squeezing by in between the stalled cars. And this with two large odd-shaped bags and weighing about 120 kilos himself! Thankfully, by the time he opened the car door, the scooter had zipped away. Generally, Dhimant also plays the role of concierge for most of our colleagues. He had web checked-in so we were just at the nick of time, but our broker friends weren't.

Worse was to follow. As soon as we somehow managed to reach the airport, one of the brokers realised that his Delhi flight was from the other terminal, KLIA2 (not KLIA1), and he had missed it.

It was complete chaos.

Dhimant could barely run due to a torn meniscus on his knee and was limping along as fast as he could manage. We were the last ones to board the flight as it geared for a take-off, and we felt our necks prickle with the glares from every passenger. But the day was not yet over. Dhimant still had to book the other broker's flight because our 'royal' brokers refused to pay for anything. Just seconds before the plane took off, Dhimant managed to send the booking confirmation to his WhatsApp number. What a relief!

It had not been an easy trip with these brokers, who wanted us to pay for everything, right from their hotel rooms to their meals. Supposedly their credit cards didn't work, despite one claiming wealth in excess of ₹1,250 crore and a plush house in Civil Lines in Delhi, adjacent to one of the famous Hindi TV cricket commentators of our times, Narottam Puri. The investor too kept us on our toes. This was meant to be a two-day visit, but it turned into a five-day saga due to his seemingly insatiable demand for new structures and proposals after each meeting. Yet the two of us were happy, because we felt once again that we had found a solution for all our problems and a window for further expansion. The investor was ready to sign an MoU of USD 350 million! Yes, you read that right!

Let's rewind a bit ...

Dr Lachhman Hirani (name changed) was the man to go to, we were told. His group boasted a big set-up with offices in across Asia, Middle East and Europe. A quick background check revealed that Hirani had his finger in many pies ... big money pies. According to multiple press releases, he had funded some government-led schemes and also been a part of massive projects worth millions of dollars. All in all, he looked like a solid party—just the one who could take a bet on our situation. Our brokers told us that Hirani was continuously travelling between countries and it was difficult to get an appointment with him, so when we came to know that he was coming to Malaysia for a few days, we rushed to meet him after somehow persuading Mr Shetty that it was a good idea and then scrambling for our visas.

'We are not just looking at loan repayment—we fund growth. I can fund you if you can show me how big you can scale up and the IPs you can build.'

These were the words from Hirani in our first meeting. He explained that our ask of USD 100 million needed some more work because there was a clause in his fund committee that stated that not more than 25% of the funded amount could be used for loan repayments. He had big ideas for us and wanted us to come up with a plan that not only saved the company but included expansion ideas. Every day after we presented a new plan, he sent us back with more homework, to look at it from different angles. Finally, after six days of work day and night and countless forecasts and data projections, he said he was ready to fund USD 350 million because Imagicaa looked like a growth option. Furthermore, given the way the Indian economy was scaling up in the discretionary space, he saw a lot of possibility. He then gave us a day's time to come up with a plan of how this USD 350 million could be deployed to meet the requirement of a stake not greater than 25% in any investee company. Further, how the invested amount would be returned in a mix of debt and equity was to be presented with a detailed cash flow statement. It felt like exam days, but way more stressful!

We would work through the night to create strategy documents, fill spreadsheets, build forecasts and debate the details with each other. We kept on with this gruelling demand

day after day because Hirani's desire for expansion lit up the light of 1% hope in us. The brokers also joined in these discussions and, frankly, though it was a demanding process, working together was motivating—we felt like we had jumped to expansion mode from survival mode.

Meeting varied people from different sections of society over the years, we had by now developed a habit of looking for clues. Hirani's office space made a statement. It was a large office in a premium area in Kuala Lumpur, a couple blocks away from Petronas Towers. It had space for his employees, a reception desk and a large corner office for him. It gave an impression of solidity and comfort.

Despite this hope, our brokers' lordly behaviour rankled. Two brokers accompanied us, and both wanted to be treated like kings. While we were very conscious of our NPA status and wanted to spend as little as possible and shared our hotel room, our brokers would not settle for anything below a four-star hotel, not rated below 4.5 on TripAdvisor or Google, wanted separate rooms with features, lavish meals and couldn't manage with a small snack in between. The credit card was spinning out of control, and there was barely anything we could do to restrain it.

Finally, on the second last day of our extended stay, Hirani gave a nod to the deal and we prepared to rush home with a signed letter of intent, a step before the MoU.

A month after our return, Mr Shetty and Mayuresh left for the second round of meetings. Dhimant could not go along as he was still recuperating from the operated knee. Just before signing, Hirani threw in a googly. He said that due diligence and valuation was mandatory before he released the funds.

Hirani gave us a list of four or five audit firms whose due diligence and valuation they would accept. Of these, almost all were the premier and internationally renowned firms like Deloitte and PWC. Seeing their names gave Mayuresh some comfort. We thought that Hirani was serious about this process. But we also knew that these well-known auditors would charge a large amount, possibly even 1 crore, and take a long time as well. Keeping our finances in mind, we chose one of the Mumbai-based local auditors in their list who had quoted ₹25 lakh as fees. In hindsight, we possibly played right into their hands.

It was a very difficult choice. On one end was an investment package of USD 350 million that would not only erase our NPA status but give us ample funds for growth and on the other end was a payment of ₹25 lakh to the auditors. It looked small in comparison to the amount we were about to get, but it was not insignificant for us at all, especially at that juncture. Undecided and still debating the validity of this idea, we signed the MoU and decided to pay for the due diligence and valuation.

Over a period of two months, we shared a ton of data with the auditors, but the second wave of COVID-19 struck, and office work again got derailed. The auditors then revealed that they were required to share the reports directly with the investors, since it was meant for *their* consumption, and the details would be released only when we paid the remaining fee. We tried very hard to get the fee reduced, but to no avail.

After the payment, the due diligence and the valuation was sent, we started waiting for a response. None came. We spoke to the brokers, but they also claimed to know nothing. Many reasons were passed around, 'the pandemic factor', 'closure of Imagicaa due to the pandemic', and 'no end in sight'.

We were quite despondent at this new blow and in our discussions, we often retraced our journey to Hirani's office—while it was a reasonably big space with cabins, conference rooms and a pantry, we realised there was nothing distinctive about it. No fixed cupboards or drawers. Everything was movable and mass-produced. Hirani could just put the shutters down and walk away anytime ... like a reality show.

But the question always remained: was he genuine?

He definitely invested in some projects; we saw media reports on his big deals from time to time. But what if out of every ten projects he got, he actually invested in only one and most went our route?

What if he had an arrangement with the local audit and valuation firm, and part of that fee was given to him? What if people like us were the fodder that kept the investment machine going?

This was the first time a scam really pinched us in the wallet—with the auditor fees and travel costs. Before that, we had managed to evade financial loss through the various scams we faced, and we avoided them all after this instance as well. We had lost hours, days, weeks and even months, but we never ever lost money. In this instance, we lost money that we could ill afford. We still have the original copy of the USD 350 million MoU we signed back in Malaysia and were loath to throw it away. But what were we going to do with that piece of paper? It had become just a piece of paper, but at that time it was so much more.

This meeting did teach us a valuable lesson. In one or two other negotiations we were again faced with the same option—choosing between auditors. The options always went like this—a whole list of internationally, well-known auditors and one—just one—Mumbai-based local auditor who we knew would charge much less than the reputed ones. It was the hope of a final solution to all monetary problems.

Would you take it?

## Scams and Shams

Sometimes, 2020 seems to be our year of scams and shams. At the very beginning, we encountered Dr Venkat and his unrealistic demands. By December, we were caught up in the trip to Malaysia. The middle of the year, however, turned into a training ground of sorts—teaching us how to distinguish between a genuine investor and a pretender.

At the same time, we were also engaged in due diligence with a potential hotel buyer from a large conglomerate, as part of the resolution plan we had presented to the lenders.

In August 2020, one of our business associates—himself a high-net-worth individual—suggested we meet Bhoopesh (name changed), describing him as a dealmaker who 'knew' the right people.

On our very first call, Bhoopesh proudly recounted his rags-to-riches story, attributing his success to sharp business acumen. In his typically dramatic style, he told us that he had purchased the very building where he had started his career more than twenty years earlier with a bank. According to him, this property would catapult him into the big league, as top cricketers were members of a club operating on the building's top floor—and the entire property was soon to go into redevelopment. He claimed that home and mortgage loans had been his ladder to success and that he now ran a flourishing agency.

Bhoopesh loved to talk, often name-dropping without pause. His hour-long calls soon became extremely painful, as he would endlessly reel off names of high-profile people from banking, the judiciary, and the who's who of Mumbai. At times, it was almost unbearable, yet we kept going with the '1% hope formula': what if, just maybe, a fraction of it was true? Sometimes, we felt we had crossed the limit of even a leap of faith, yet we could not bring ourselves to stop trying.

Bhoopesh's confidence after these discussions often bordered on arrogance. He behaved as though he already owned Imagicaa, and he would magnanimously declare that he would keep our jobs, allow us to remain in the company and even reward us. As if …

Bhoopesh always came with unreasonable demands. He wanted a 50% stake in the company, along with an upfront fee of ₹25 crore—over and above the equity! But his list of wants didn't stop there. He also insisted on a bonus mandate: for example, if the banks agreed to settle at ₹500 crore (while he planned to bring in investors for ₹650 crore), then he would pocket 50% of the difference as well. His demands were so excessive that even the old style of 'Pathaan funding' would have sounded far more reasonable in comparison.

As discussions went on, his demands only grew bolder. He began asking for free stays at our hotel for himself and his family, under the convenient excuse of 'investor visits' and 'recces'. From experience, we had learnt that such requests were the hallmark of sham investors and brokers, not professionals. Genuine investors rarely asked for free accommodation. Their priority was usually to assess the property and the destination, observe the customer footfall, evaluate risks, meet key team members and then leave—ideally before city traffic worsened. Yet, despite our growing suspicions, we decided to eliminate any bias and give him the benefit of doubt by visiting his office.

A visit to Bhoopesh's office immediately revealed his obsession with projecting influence. The walls were lined with photographs of him posing with corporate leaders, Bollywood celebrities, government officials and other public figures. It was meant to impress, but we had a habit of reading between the lines whenever we met people. That day, our instincts sharpened as we noticed the inconsistencies.

After a brief conversation, Bhoopesh asked us to wait outside while he entertained other clients. From the outer room, we studied his office closely. He boasted of having 150 chartered accountants working under him, but there was no evidence of such scale. The few people around looked, spoke and behaved more like small-time loan sales agents. The cramped office could barely fit ten people, and the only writing on his meeting room whiteboard displayed basic sales targets, not financial strategies. This left us questioning what his business truly was.

While sitting there, we felt vibrations beneath us and a faint rumbling sound. After the meeting, curiosity made us insist on finding the source. We walked down the lane, and as we circled around the building, we discovered that it directly abutted the Western Railway tracks, near Charni Road station. The vibrations, of course, came from passing trains. It was yet another clue: the building had likely been purchased at a throwaway price, and any redevelopment here would pose near-impossible challenges with the authorities.

Our interactions with Bhoopesh lasted barely two months, but it quickly became evident that this association had no future. Beyond name-dropping and displaying arrogance, he had no substance—no proposal for the banks, no concrete strategy and no real connections where they mattered: at the ground or middle-management levels.

The final nail in the coffin came when we researched him online. On Facebook, we came across two profiles—one under the name 'Bhoopesh' and another as 'Bhupesh'. Further digging revealed they were indeed the same person. We then discovered that Bhupesh had been charged in a loan-related case a few years ago, a past that likely explained the sudden change in his name spelling. That revelation sealed our decision. We stopped interacting with him altogether.

## The Rainbow Delusion

In September of the same year, we were both stunned when we received a formally written letter of intent to invest in Imagicaa from a firm we had never engaged with before. The most astonishing part of the offer was a strict condition: 'We will pay the banks the entire amount.'

No previous investor had ever insisted on such a clause. In fact, most investors typically hunted for a cheaper way to clear the company's debt. Negotiations usually began with questions like, 'How much discount can we get?' or 'What is the possible haircut on the debt settlement?'. This new approach left us both curious and suspicious. What was this firm's angle?

Even though we found the condition implausible, the fact that the offer arrived via a formal email to our official IDs compelled us to explore it. Before the meeting, they sent us a WhatsApp message explaining that they had signed MoUs with a state government to invest ₹4,000 crore at a state investment summit, and included photos of themselves standing with dignitaries at the event. All this correspondence created the impression that they had abundant funds to invest, and finally, we might have a legitimate investor who had reached out directly and formally.

Still, one question loomed large: Where was their money coming from?

The meeting, however, was anticlimactic. Two very ordinary-looking individuals—Anandkumar and Chawan—walked into our office. They looked like people you'd find on a local Mumbai train. Their appearance failed to match the image they had projected of high-profile, deep-pocketed investors. Anandkumar wore a basic blue suit and tie, while Chawan, claimed to be a medical doctor who had worked at the BMC before joining the investment group. Neither of them exhibited any signs of significant wealth.

They explained, 'Our fund's guidelines do not allow us to finance an NPA, which is why we want to pay the banks in full.' This meant they needed the loan account to be regularised by paying all arrears before taking over the company. But given that Imagicaa had been classified as an NPA since 2018, we wondered how this would actually work.

Anandkumar and Chawan further claimed that if all lenders were paid in full, the transaction would be considered a 'refinance' rather than an NPA settlement. They went on to say that they owned around 10,000 acres of land near Nalsarovar in Gujarat and that Disney World officials had conducted site visits there. After our meeting, they began discussing possible deal structures.

But who were they, really? What funds were they actually representing? We had no idea.

They provided the name of a Russian-sounding holding company and assured us the source of their money was 'non-criminal'. The only positive sign was that, unlike Dr Venkat, they seemed to understand what is possible for a listed company. We began negotiations and started discussing details of the MoU.

During these discussions, we started researching their backgrounds. No mention of their names or their company existed online. We checked the state government website to verify their claimed MoUs from the investment summit; again, nothing appeared. Digging deeper, we examined a press clipping they had sent with their photographs at the summit—but we could not find any such article or image anywhere. That's when our suspicions deepened. With the help of a colleague, we closely inspected the picture and discovered that it had been photoshopped.

Once discovered, the manipulation was glaringly obvious—we wondered how we had missed it in the first place.

We still don't know what scamsters like them hoped to gain from this. Was it just their two minutes of fame? Could it be something else entirely?

Perhaps they genuinely believed their investors would deliver—or maybe they were victims of a scam themselves. There were simply too many unanswered questions.

*Amigo Mantra #19:* Kaise milte hain. *You will meet all kinds, just stay focused!*

*Amigo Mantra #20:* Har waqt kuch kehta hai. *Enjoy the journey at each step and be observant!*

# Thought #7: The Underground World of Brokers

Our trusted aide, Amarnath, usually acted as the first filter—or more accurately, a key sourcing funnel. He would hold lengthy discussions with brokers, informing them of our funding requirements, the basic working structure of a listed company, and our expectations regarding commissions. When he felt they were credible enough, he would introduce them to us. Over the course of four years, we must have met around sixty brokers and signed twelve term sheets or reached near-signing stages—but none ultimately came through. We often wonder about the many more brokers he must have turned away, considering even the ones we finally met came with so many stories.

As we met more brokers on our journey, we gradually began to untangle some recurring patterns that could help us predict how they would behave.

The first conversation with brokers was always about their commission percentage. They showed no interest in understanding what a business turnaround entailed. None had industry knowledge or could provide even a basic briefing note, let alone any financial analysis. A few tossed around some vague tips on strategic planning (such as during the Malaysia trip and with Guruji) or marketing.

Usually, the broker chains were long and frustrating to break. Mayuresh experienced this first hand with Dr Venkat. More often than not, the broker we met was the tenth person in a long chain and was very reluctant to connect us to the key source. Brokers never revealed the name of the primary financier, though that financier was always presented to us as a 'credible party'. Everyone seemed to believe that revealing any more details would cut into their commission.

When we finally secured a meeting with this 'credible party', business etiquette dictated no exchange of business cards. Sharing cards was seen as an act of betrayal because the individual we met was often merely the last link in a long chain starting from the investor. In that room, brokers had already mentally divided portions of the deal among themselves, so you walked into initial meetings trailing a chain of brokers.

Many first-time brokers mistakenly assumed their job was done once they arranged a meeting with an investor. They would start discussing numbers right away. We always made it clear that commissions would be paid only upon deal closure. There was no other way to work with us.

Our experience with multiple brokers taught us that it's better to work on a success-based commission model rather than fixed rates or mandates because many deals fall apart even after signing an MoU. Also, engaging with too many brokers simultaneously risks stretching your bandwidth and spoiling a genuine deal.

In this murky world of brokering, we've seen people quote ₹1,100 crore as the 'sales value', of which as much as ₹200 crore would be their charges. It is a farce that brokers not only demand commissions but also position themselves as equity holders.

As our acquaintances in this brokering world grew, we too began using WhatsApp groups to keep abreast of ongoing negotiations. Even today, Dhimant keeps those groups on his phone under umbrella names like Imagicaa World, Imagicaa Strategy, Imagicaa Joint Venture and many more.

# 8

# From Bids to Bedlam

*'This is a disaster, there are no bids ... Get Murli!'*

In July 2021, the two of us found ourselves in the midst of a frantic situation. Bankers were calling us incessantly with one pressing question: 'Where is the bid from Murli Vaman of Dreamworld Media?'

This was our second auction, and it was not unfolding as the bankers had planned. In fact, it seemed that nothing leading up to the auction had gone as expected.

Back in December 2020, we received a call from Mr Shetty, who informed us that a well-known hotelier had mentioned a big international investor staying at his hotel in Kharghar. Mr Shetty appeared very enthusiastic and positive about this investor, so much so that he relaxed his strict pandemic no-meet policy. Even when we met him previously for important discussions or updates at his residence, he insisted on double masking and maintaining an extraordinary social distance of nearly 15 feet.

Yet, for this meeting, Mr Shetty was willing to leave his house and come to our office. It seemed as though we had finally found someone genuine, given the risk Mr Shetty was prepared to take.

## A Hat-Trick

The first meeting almost didn't happen. We were scheduled to meet at 3 p.m., but our big international investor, Murli Vaman, founder of Dreamworld Media (not to be mistaken for Steven Spielberg), finally sauntered in around 5.30 p.m.

Tired of waiting and needing to attend an urgent bank meeting, Mayuresh had already left. Dhimant also left for another meeting, having been told by a colleague that the meeting was postponed to another day. As luck would have it, within half an hour of our departure, Murli arrived. Our teammates called us urgently, and we rushed back. That's when we realised it was also Mr Shetty's first meeting with him.

Incidentally, this was a sign of things to come: no meeting with Murli ever started on time. He was always late and never apologetic, even when bankers were kept waiting. His attitude seemed to be, '*Mein der karta nahin, der ho jaati hai.* (I don't delay; delays just happen!) Deal with it.' It was as if he took pleasure in making people wait, especially when he knew they were desperate.

On that first day, Dhimant walked into the meeting room visibly annoyed by the delay. But Murli's first appearance left us utterly gobsmacked. Tall, with long hair, a face heavily made up, deep red lipstick, a thick gold chain around his neck, dressed entirely in black—including hat, blazer, T-shirt, trousers and shoes—he looked like the antithesis of a seasoned investor or businessperson.

We didn't know what to make of him. Most people we met were shrewd yet soft-spoken professionals or businessmen:

mild-mannered and conformist in their attire. Murli was the opposite—never soft-spoken; his presence was loud. Here's a sample from one of our conversations:

'I want to own your business tomorrow,' Murli declared.

'Yes, it's possible. You can pay the entire outstanding principal of ₹1,000 crore and any dues, and with the necessary procedures, the company can change hands,' Dhimant replied.

'That's easy. I will get that done,' said Murli.

'Are you certain? You may not have to pay in full,' Mayuresh intervened, trying to bring reason to the absurd dialogue. 'The banks are willing to settle closer to enterprise value, which means a haircut. You can discuss this with them.'

We always shared the full picture with interested investors. At that time, we had a very solid investor waiting in the wings—the Malpani Group, who eventually acquired Imagicaa. The Malpani-led consortium was principally ready to pay ₹575 crore, closer to the enterprise value as determined by a valuer. The banks wanted a value higher than enterprise value, although they had no other investors in the pipeline and we were in the middle of the pandemic. There were barely any buyers.

'It doesn't matter to me. I can pay ₹1,600 crore ... and even more,' said Murli.

Mayuresh's suggestion of a haircut seemed beneath Murli's dignity. He just shook his ponytail dismissively and waved aside the idea, as if the additional ₹1,025 crore was inconsequential.

The rest of the discussions continued in this surreal way. Nothing seemed to faze him—he only wanted to give us money to pay lenders. He did not want control over management, nor to build Imagicaa. His plan was to create a huge VFX studio in our park and make money from there. Murli said he had run a VFX studio in Hollywood called Dreamworld and considered himself a wizard at it. He kept claiming that he knew many people ready to invest in his projects.

In all our discussions, he never asked about the business numbers. When Dhimant tried to fill him in, Murli just shrugged and said the VFX business was so large it didn't matter what the park generated.

We simply couldn't believe the man—or his behaviour.

Murli was a stark contrast to any previous engagement. His ways were weird, un-businesslike, almost unreal. That's why we weren't convinced. Still, Mr Shetty held onto that 1% Hope principle and didn't dismiss Murli's story and potential.

Seeing Dhimant's utter displeasure and discomfort, Mr Shetty likely anticipated that Dhimant might express his honest opinion at this critical juncture. Known for his upfront, no-nonsense approach, Dhimant's straightforwardness is well-known.

For the first time since joining Imagicaa, Mr Shetty took Dhimant aside into his cabin and urged him to stay calm, drawing on his vast experience:

'Dhimant, don't do anything rash. Murli might become your next boss,' he said.

That stunned us both. Mr Shetty seemed genuinely hopeful, maybe even positive, that this deal would go through.

Meanwhile, we felt Murli was a completely phony character. We just couldn't connect with him. It felt like we were missing something critical. Perhaps the idea of building a VFX studio had clouded his judgement, given how close it was to his heart.

Thus, we decided to give this another shot and keep an open mind, though we remained reluctant. This was the first and only time we didn't want to move forward with the 1% hope theory. We were both deeply concerned about the possible impact this conversation could have on the promising talks with the Malpani Group.

Dhimant advised Mr Shetty to tell Murli to contact the banks directly and that we should completely distance ourselves from him. Mr Shetty was not pleased with this suggestion. Seeing our reluctance to refer Murli to the banks, he directed Murli to an investment banker who had access to the banks' recovery teams so he could make an introduction and share his offer.

From that point on, it became the banks' prerogative to evaluate the investor and his proposal. It was the right move, as we couldn't reject Murli's bid outright. Doing so could have reflected poorly on our cooperation and intentions.

## Freebies and More

Murli Vaman now wanted to visit Imagicaa, which is normal practice for most investors. However, we were soon to realise that drama was an essential ingredient in every meeting with Murli.

We were travelling through low-connectivity areas and couldn't receive his calls, so slightly miffed, he impatiently called Mr Shetty to arrange a visit and stay at Imagicaa for himself, his son and a friend. This request raised our suspicions because we had seen similar behaviour with Bhoopesh. Murli's timing was even more questionable—it was during a COVID-19 wave, when there were no crowds, the rides were not operating, and many team members were absent. What exactly did he expect to see or assess?

At the bankers' insistence, Mr Shetty arranged for our senior architect to be on hand to show the premises from the perspective of creating a studio and to explain the overall plan for Imagicaa. The park spans 110 acres and includes a theme park filled with rollercoasters and rides for children and adults, a waterpark and a snow park. It's a vast area that takes hours to explore. Most serious investors usually toured the entire park to understand the value their money would unlock, especially through the pandemic.

'It's ok,' was Murli's entire review after a brief ten-minute walk around the park. He had kept the senior architect waiting for around four hours before finally descending, walking ten steps and retreating to his room. For the next few days, he simply stayed in the hotel, enjoying the facilities with his son and friend.

By then, we were morc than convinced that Murli was not the genuine investor he claimed to be.

## Extravagant Assertions

Having voluntarily stepped back from interactions with Murli and leaving the matter to the bankers, the two of us were absent when Murli met with them. Later, we heard snippets of the meeting from the investment banker who accompanied Murli and watched in shock as the scene unfolded.

Bank consortium meetings are usually attended by junior and mid-level bank employees. Only the lead bank typically sends a senior representative, often at the AGM or DGM level. In some meetings, bankers strategise to negotiate better settlements for NPA accounts. Usually, company representatives are excluded from such meetings, as bankers prefer in-camera discussions. Especially in cases involving management change, bankers prefer meeting only the investor to avoid any conflict of interest. Thus, in this meeting, only Murli was called, with the investment banker present solely to provide any necessary financial details—which Murli never needed.

*Bankers: A return of ₹575 crore is insufficient for the amount we have lent.*

*Murli: Ok, how much do you want?*

*Bankers: We think ₹725 crore is a fair valuation.*

*Murli: That's no problem. I can easily arrange it.*

Such a sudden and substantial increase shocked the investment banker. His grim assessment was, '*Ya to pagal hai, ya bahut paise hain*'. (He is either crazy or very rich).

All previous discussions with investors and fund houses had grudgingly led the banks to accept a valuation of ₹575 crore purely from a mathematical standpoint—which translated to roughly a 40% haircut. Murli's response discarded that number outright and presented a superior option in an instant. He had positioned himself overnight as the perfect solution—and everyone wants a solution like that.

*Bankers: How quickly can you arrange the funds?*

*Murli: I can get the funds soon; they are parked abroad.*

*Bankers: Can you get them in ninety days?*

*Murli: I can get them in thirty days!*

*It seemed there was nothing Murli couldn't do.*

*Murli: The funds are in Hong Kong.*

*Bankers (among themselves): Will we be able to get the funds from Hong Kong? (At that time, Hong Kong investments were stuck awaiting RBI approval.)*

*Murli: That doesn't matter. I'll get the funds from Dubai or California.*

Some bankers, we were told, remained sceptical and pressed him for proof of funds and details about how he would access the money. However, most representatives were pleased by the higher valuation and curtly dismissed the doubters. A better number sounded impressive to their seniors and board, and could help allay fears of a vigilance inquiry.

Hearing this shocking conversation, the two of us decided to take firm action and convey our concerns to the entire consortium. We wanted to put on record that we did not approve this deal without due diligence or concrete commitment. Another worry was that because of Murli's scam-like behaviour, we might lose the Malpanis' interest. They had waited patiently for nearly four years, and this could make them walk away.

In a rare moment of anger, Mayuresh drafted and sent an email to the bankers stating that we had no valid proof of Murli's credentials and that no proper diligence had been done as customary, and concluded by saying we did not recommend him to the banks. It would, therefore, be unwise to rely on him. Dhimant fully agreed, and we sent the email like a bazooka blast.

But you know what happens when you try to tell the truth sometimes? People get angry.

'Why the hell did you send that mail? Don't you want us to get a good deal? You must recall it now,' demanded a senior banker angrily—one of the fastest responses ever from the Recovery department. My bazooka shot back with double the intensity.

'But sir, I copied it to twenty people. It was intended as a caution and for awareness. Further, we truly don't know Murli or his ability to consummate this transaction,' Mayuresh tried to reason.

'I don't care. RECALL THE EMAIL,' was his curt response.

Given the delicate situation, the roles reversed. Dhimant sent a milder email clarifying our view, stating that the banks were welcome to work with Murli to recover dues, and that company management would fully cooperate with any recovery efforts by the lenders.

## It's a NO Deal

A few months after that ill-fated consortium meeting, we found ourselves helplessly answering repeated calls from bankers who kept pressing Murli to make his bid. Murli, when contacted, seemed completely unfazed.

'I have the funds. It will just take a day or two more to arrive. This is not a major delay—the RBI regulations are just taking longer than expected,' he said with his usual nonchalance.

Even after the auction failed and the bankers urged him to at least deposit the earnest money, he continued offering the same excuses. 'The funds are on their way. I just need a few more days. It's not my problem that the funds are delayed.'

Our first auction was an open auction where banks did not set a reserve price, using price discovery to possibly achieve a better amount than anticipated. During the second auction, however, based on Murli's conversations, the bankers set a reserve price of ₹725 crore. This amount discouraged some serious bidders, such as the Malpani Group, since it was much higher than what they were willing to pay.

For us, it was not only a complete waste of time but something far worse. That failed auction set a new benchmark in the system—₹725 crore. We also had to grapple with the fallout of genuine investors feeling ignored and undervalued by the bankers.

## The Freebie Scam

Most of our peers are professionals. They operate from offices and interact with other professionals. None of us had ever dealt with this murky side of human behaviour. Of course, we had all heard stories of frauds and scams, but always *about* fraudsters—never coming face to face with one like this.

One question that constantly plagued us was: what do scamsters like Murli gain from all this? We were not a cash-rich company; we were simply looking for a way out of our NPA crisis. What did he gain from this 'dreamworld' of bluffs he built? Was all the rigmarole—the blustering, the freebies like unpaid stays at Imagicaa and other hotels—truly worth it?

Soon after the failed auction, the façade Murli had constructed began to crumble. A newspaper article alerted us to Murli's other scams. He had managed a free stay of five or six months at a hotel in Kharghar (near Mumbai) by telling the owner he was the next owner of Imagicaa. True to his extravagant ways, the bill reportedly ballooned to ₹25 lakh. To evade payment, Murli and his pre-teen son made a dramatic exit via the drainpipes, according to news reports.

Printed from
THE TIMES OF INDIA

**Navi Mumbai: Man runs up Rs 25 lakh hotel bill, slips out of bathroom**

TNN | Sep 3, 2021, 10.24 AM IST

Whenever we thought of his son—whom Dhimant had met twice in our office—we were reminded of Leonardo DiCaprio's character in the famous Hollywood movie *Catch Me If You Can*. Just as DiCaprio's character learnt the tricks of scamming from his conman father, this young child seemed to be learning the art of conning from Murli. We sincerely hope Murli's son chooses a better path in life rather than following in his father's footsteps.

Next, we heard that Murli had again used his 'charm' and self-created evidence to convince builders and real estate owners that he was purchasing Imagicaa. These stories helped him gain easy access to an expensive apartment worth ₹4–5 crore. On one occasion, however, his fabricated tale fell flat—when the marketing head of a highly reputed builder, who happened to be a friend, called us to verify Murli's claim.

We soon dubbed this the 'freebie scam'. As we reflected on how everything had gone so wrong, we realised that scamsters like Murli operate in a grey zone, promising the world but delivering nothing, while squeezing every possible fringe freebie they can get. They live in a false dream. It was no coincidence that Murli's fictitious company was called Dreamworld.

To understand what allowed Murli and others like him to get away with the pipedreams they promised, we began listing his actions and behaviours from the time he first met us, searching for any pattern or modus operandi connecting him to other scamsters like Bhoopesh and more whom we encountered. Murli, of course, stood miles ahead in this dubious category.

First, they always insisted on taking pictures with well-known people. Murli demanded a picture with Mr Shetty during our first meeting and, true to character, requested that we edit the lighting in the image before sharing it with him. Most scamsters we met wanted photographs with big names—it built credibility for them. Bhoopesh hung such pictures in his office; Murli showed his to others to prove his links with Mr Shetty. These photos helped establish their authenticity and lure unsuspecting victims.

Second, they always projected arrogance and total command. Khan and Murli were no exceptions. Their *khandani raisi wala andaaz*—an air of old wealth and confidence—served as a protective shield, preventing victims from noticing the gap between reality and their image.

Third, they always provided answers people desperately wanted to hear. No number was too high for them. They understood a fundamental human trait: the desire for a better option. None of the scamsters we met—Khan, Bhoopesh, the Vibgyor team, Murli (and others we won't name here)—ever flinched at financial figures. They were always ready with the 'cash'. Murli's meeting with the lender consortium was a masterclass in this tactic. He knew the rigid hierarchy within banks. No one wanted to be the bearer of bad news, but everyone wanted to carry tidings of a profit.

The poor, gullible victims usually ended up financing the scamsters' lavish lifestyles or becoming yet another piece of evidence for future cons—a Ponzi scheme aimed at extracting freebies: a hotel suite beyond their means, a house they can't pay for, a lifestyle they desperately desire. Our failed auction was a mere fallout of Murli's antics.

Murli was not the only one attempting such scams, but he went the farthest with his stunts. The others we caught and deflected early. Murli broke through barriers and gained access to the bankers, wreaking havoc and nearly ruining the transaction that later turned Imagicaa around.

That's why, ever since, whenever anyone readily accedes to any demand, we become deeply suspicious.

Once bitten, twice shy. Here, we had been bitten many times.

*Amigo Mantra #21: Everything is 'possible' for the one who has no money.*

*Amigo Mantra #22: Money is a by-product for those who have no product to begin with.*

## Thought #8: The Problem of Sticky Numbers

In our NCLT journey, there were many critical 'be-vigilant' points—moments that could ensure our survival for another day or abruptly knock us out of the process. Unfortunately, we often discovered these points only in hindsight. This journey had no descriptive travelogue to politely steer us in the right direction or warn us of fast-moving rapids, lurking dangers or man-eating sharks.

One major learning was understanding that the number lenders hold is absolutely critical. They have some indicative target or break-even number below which they will not deal. We, of course, never knew that exact number, but we gradually began to grasp the range of enterprise values they considered acceptable.

The easiest way for banks to decide on this number is to leave the decision to the judiciary in NCLT courts. This way, they avoid direct involvement in valuation and shield themselves from fears that their 'given number' might be dredged up years later—even post-retirement—during inquiries by agencies like the CBI, ED, SFIO or RBI. These fears are real because they have happened to bankers in the past. That's why, when fund houses or investment bankers offered very low numbers and shrugged with 'What choice do the banks have?'—we wanted to say that, for some bankers, this company was just a file. Why would they risk inquiries by their seniors or regulators by approving any low number, no matter how realistic? It wasn't easy for the bankers either—*karo to dikkat, no karo to kisi aur ko dikkat* (do it, and it's a problem; if you don't do it, someone else has a problem). Among them, we did meet some truly brave bankers who faced these challenges fearlessly and sincerely, but for most, it was just another day in paradise.

Our first valuation in 2018 was ₹1,100 crore by an agency seemingly intent on impressing lenders, bringing the number closer to book value. This figure became the first sticky number we had to contend with. Every investor and fund manager received this number, but some, especially those keenly interested, did their own valuations and arrived at numbers they were comfortable paying. Often, a 50% gap existed between the bank's sticky number and fund managers' valuations of Imagicaa. Initially, banks were reluctant to settle for such low returns, and thus talks stalled—the gap was a very tall order to bridge.

In 2019, the second sticky number appeared when, propelled by Rahul Manwani, Mr Shetty handled a ₹650 crore offer to the lead bank.

By January 2021, with no other genuine options, bankers grudgingly began to accept a more feasible number based on scientific valuations by seasoned valuers. The valuation was slowly aligning with reality, and the banks conducted nearly one valuation annually, though we were never fully informed of the exact numbers.

Then Murli Vaman entered the scene, casting his intangible spell. Suddenly, the banks believed they had found a much better number. While the Malpani Group was assembling all the requisites and tangibles for a transaction already on the table, Murli had only his words and dreams. His ₹725 crore offer became the third sticky number we struggled to fend off.

Murli's Dreamworld created a significant problem—not only for that auction but for many months afterward—because it created a number that stuck in the system. Bankers began demanding ₹725 crore instead of ₹575 crore, which itself was 25–30% higher than any other investor or fund was willing to pay. (For context, Aion had offered ₹450 crore in 2019.) Sadly, no one could meet that inflated number—least of all Murli—but the new number was entrenched in the banking system. Bankers expected the same from other buyers despite the failed auction.

Our greatest fear was that, to avoid controversy, someone might simply say, 'Let NCLT decide.' That would undo all our painstaking efforts.

It was astonishing at times how the media seemed perfectly in sync with the developments taking place in the resolution process. On several occasions, we learnt the discussed numbers from media reports rather than from other stakeholders. In a couple of instances, we were surprised by the level of detail in the articles—details that could only have come from someone with direct or indirect access to internal confidential documents.

# 9

# Before the Gavel's Final Fall

*'You need to pay 5% processing fees. 1% at the time of MoU and 4% deducted at the time of disbursement.'*

By June 2021, we had been battling NPA and navigating the NCLT process since 2018, enduring two failed auctions. Time was running out. In fact, the pandemic—which had brought us to our knees by shutting down the operational park completely and cutting off its income—ironically helped us stay in the NCLT court process a little longer. The March 2020 court hearing, where we were nearly admitted into NCLT, could not have been prolonged this way if not for courts limiting hearings to only the most urgent cases.

Because of COVID-19 restrictions, our hotel became our only income generator, albeit operating at 50% capacity. Still, we managed to pay staff and maintain the park using GST refunds, a cutback corpus, VAT refunds and marketing campaigns offering highly discounted Imagicaa tickets with promises of visitation once the parks reopened.

One early morning in June, the two of us rushed to the Maharashtra State Electricity Board (MSEB) headquarters because our hotel's power supply had been disconnected and it was running only on a generator, which would soon run out of fuel. With a few guests in the hotel, a blackout was unaffordable.

Soon, it became clear that no one there was paying attention to us. Clerks told us to provide documents proving minimum consumption at the hotel and park, then made us sit outside. Fortunately, Mayuresh is a veritable bank of documents and managed to find precisely what was needed—a godsend in situations demanding proof.

It turned out that the MSEB had sent a disconnection notice fourteen days prior—but we only received it one day before because it was sent to the wrong email ID. That left us with far too little time to act.

The government had introduced a scheme early in the COVID-19 crisis allowing industries to pay their power dues in EMIs. Our last EMI was delayed, resulting in electricity disconnection. We were told the scheme was now closed, as the lockdown had ended and industries had reopened. We tried explaining that Imagicaa remained closed since entertainment venues were not allowed to open.

No one was willing to listen, and after hours of waiting to present our case, Dhimant raised his voice while speaking with the hotel management to inquire about the power situation: '*Diesel kitna bacha hai generator mein*? *Abhi kya hai power situation*?' ('How much diesel is left? What's the power situation now?')

He was as loud as possible to get their attention. Around 7 p.m., we were finally called into a meeting.

One official angrily demanded, 'Why should we give you reprieve? You broke the rules. If you are driving on the road and break the rules, you are a violator.'

Mayuresh was enraged by this irrelevant remark. We were the victims here, yet being treated like criminals was unimaginable.

They gave us two options: go to court or pay our bills. 'If you don't pay, others will follow,' was their reasoning.

'But others are not closed like us,' we countered.

Finally, by 8 p.m.—we had arrived at 11 a.m.—they told us we had to pay around ten EMIs plus one missed payment. Since the EMI scheme was over, they decided we had to pay the entire outstanding amount upfront. The only concession, after much pleading, was allowing us to pay this sum in three EMIs, putting immense pressure on our already precarious cash flow. We were completely arm-twisted, though they made it sound like we had a choice. It was an ideal example of Hobson's choice.

We had no option but to agree and get the power restored. At 11 p.m., after ensuring the hotel's power was restored, we left the MSEB office. It had been a long day of battling bureaucratic red tape and rigid regulations.

## Who's Come Calling?

During this uncertain time, after the second auction, a broker from one of our investor visits, Deepak, contacted Mayuresh again. In fact, he had been one of the brokers on our Malaysia trip and had kept in touch. He would randomly call, asking, '*Haanji sirji, aagey kuch ho raha hai? Is baar mere paas ek pakki deal hai.*' ('Yes sir, is there any progress? I have a confirmed deal this time.') This time, he added that he had an interested party who wanted to meet us urgently. Upon further probing, he gave bare details: the investor was a parliamentarian—a man of few words—and wanted to meet ALL of us in the first meeting, as time was of the essence.

We sounded off Mr Shetty, who a little reluctantly agreed to an urgent meeting, and we waited for this 'investor'.

On the day of the meeting, Deepak arrived at our office accompanied by a very stern-faced gentleman in a dapper suit. Deepak introduced him as Sanjay Aggarwal. Sanjay carried himself like a senior government official, wearing a tailored Nehru jacket, crisp white shirt and shiny patent leather shoes. Every step and glance exuded authority.

From the outset, Sanjay took charge. He marched into the room, scrutinised everything and everyone, and sat down saying, 'Let's get down to the details pointwise. I will handle the banks with my method.' His attitude was curt, probing and business-like. The seriousness he radiated was so intense that later Mayuresh said it felt more like an Enforcement Directorate investigation than a fund-raising discussion.

We explained everything in detail and shared the requested documents. As the first half of the meeting concluded, Dhimant escorted Sanjay to the restroom, and his aura softened. From behind the stern façade emerged a boastful statement: 'If you know of more deals like this, let me know. We have a lot of money.'

This behaviour was so out of character it stopped Dhimant in his tracks. Yet, with no other option, and the 1% hope mantra still alive, he carried on. Later, Sanjay was insistent—almost persistent—that he be invited to Mr Shetty's home for dinner or at least high tea. 'That's how we build relationships. Sitting at home is better than discussing in a hotel. *Hum rishta banate hain business mein, tab baat banti hai.*' ('We form relationships in business. That's when deals can get done.')

Mr Shetty politely refused every request, and Sanjay's persistence began to feel uncomfortable. How many times can one say no politely before the message is clear?

Finally, we all agreed to have the evening discussion at the club with Mr Shetty.

Mr Shetty follows a strict regimen, is particular about his schedule and rarely misses his evening tennis, which keeps him fit despite the stress and 'justifies' his evening drink. That day, too, he chose to catch his tennis session and asked us to schedule the follow-up meeting around 7 p.m.

Deepak and Sanjay joined us at the club. The two of us planned to steer the conversation towards the deal, but Sanjay had different ideas. 'How are you making the onion pakoras?' he asked the staff. 'I want you to dip the onion for just a few minutes before putting them in boiling oil. Don't let them soak in the masala for too long.'

Sanjay's off-track conversation left us completely bemused. We didn't know how to react.

Barely had the waiter left, when Sanjay had another sudden idea. He wanted us to move to the far end of the swimming pool. By then, Mr Shetty had joined us and seemed close to losing what little patience he had left. Deepak looked at us for support

regarding Sanjay's new request. We quietly moved, hoping the conversation would get back on track.

The main transactional discussion was brief, and the meeting soon concluded. Given the deal's time pressures, we agreed to visit Deepak and Sanjay at their hotel to iron out the finer points of the draft MoU and simultaneously try to understand the identity of the actual financiers.

At the hotel, Sanjay told us he was part of the board of a trust or fund that acted as investors for their clients. He said the board would meet in a few days, which was why he had come urgently to Mumbai to understand our requirements.

All this sounded plausible, but what didn't seem right was the complete change in Sanjay. He now resembled a prosperous North Delhi businessman rather than the strict government official from the morning. Once in the hotel room, Sanjay and Deepak changed into more comfortable clothes. Sanjay chose a T-shirt with eye-popping colours and ragged track pants. We certainly did not expect someone claiming to be the deciding voice of a fund worth thousands of crore to dress so casually.

Our belief in them began to fade, but we worked late into the night, detailing feasible points for the MoU. Despite a long day, we felt a sense of accomplishment for steering the conversation in the right direction and gaining a clear sense of a potential transaction. The morning's awkward pakora and high-tea conversation and Mr Shetty's growing impatience were not as important now that we had movement in the right direction.

Deepak, the broker, urged us to get the term sheet signed at the earliest, so we spent half the night working out details.

Morning brought fresh challenges. Sanjay visited our office but was reluctant to sign the MoU, which outlined the company's liabilities, transaction contours and investor requirements as represented by Sanjay and Deepak. Everything had been previously discussed, but Sanjay insisted that only Mr Shetty should sign the document and refused to sign it himself. Dhimant immediately objected, stating we needed a countersigned document for our records. After side discussions, they finally agreed that Mrs Aggarwal would sign because she was a trustee of the fund.

By this point, we were convinced this was another write-off.

Later, a finance team member told us that both Deepak and Sanjay had requested cabin-sized luggage to carry some large coffee-table books about the park's making, which Mr Shetty had graciously gifted them at our first meeting.

They spoke of crore yet couldn't afford bags worth a few thousand rupees.

It seemed like a cheap extension of a freebie scam, and we tore up the mandate paper Sanjay had gotten Mr Shetty to sign.

By then, we were certain no more Murli-like characters would be allowed to shadow our turnaround journey.

**Deja Vu**

To counteract the negative fallout from the second failed auction, both of us were asked to start searching for more investors. That's how, in August 2021, the two of us found ourselves meeting a financer, Nagendra Yadav (name changed), in the sleepy bylanes of Sanpada. Yadav was recommended by a broker who had been part of a long chain of unconnected brokers and had previously taken us to meet an interested financer whose deal never materialised. Usually, in such meetings, no numbers are shared, so Kamble—this broker—spent time searching for us on Facebook and Google until he finally tracked down Mayuresh's number.

'*Mayuresh sir, aap aao, ye genuine guy hai, hamare gaon ke*,' he said after introducing himself. ('Mayuresh sir, you come. This guy is genuine, from my village.')

Kamble was straightforward and uncomplicated, unlike Panse and some other brokers we had spoken with.

'*Business toh maine unke saath kabhi kiya nahi, but I've heard ye finance karte hain. I can get you to sit, phir aap assess karlo whether it works for you or not. Hoga toh mujhe mere paise de do.*' ('I have never done business with them, but I've heard that they are into financing. I can set up a meeting, then you assess yourself whether it works for you or not. You can pay me if it works out.')

Mayuresh was initially uninterested, but since the place was on our way and Kamble had sent some screenshots, we decided to give it a try. After the first meeting, Kamble didn't need to hard-sell it because it ticked some boxes in our minds. Nagendra Yadav had a decent-sized office, and we saw some well-known people conversing with him. The best part was that he asked all the right questions:

- How are you going to repay the loan?
- Show me the cash flows.
- Show me the projections.
- What business have you done last year?

We had been asked so many irrelevant questions by others that these substantive queries made us feel we were moving in the right direction. Mayuresh answered in detail and compiled a file of all the relevant documents. He was clearly at home here. Another positive sign was that Yadav's office 'NY Finance Pvt. Ltd' had an NBFC license, which we verified online. At the time, most NBFCs were understandably hesitant to deal with us. Yadav, however, said he specialised in funding stressed assets.

In one meeting, Yadav requested to meet Mr Shetty, who surprisingly agreed to accompany us next time. It was a very cordial meeting, and Yadav posed for a picture, presenting Mr Shetty with a shawl. His hooded, secretive eyes contrasted with the pristine white shawl. Yadav told Mr Shetty he wanted to add both of our names to the term sheet as recipients. 'I can make out these guys are committed. I know I will get my money back from them.'

Yadav also brought an ex-banker on board, claiming the banker would provide invaluable help navigating discussions with the banks due to his inside knowledge. We were somewhat surprised, since Yadav already had an NBFC and should technically know what bankers want.

At Yadav's office, we often noticed a man named Terry (name changed) in another room, speaking animatedly on the phone. We often caught snippets of him discussing external commercial borrowings (ECBs) or USD 100 million coming from Dubai. This was music to our ears, as we realised we needed someone knowledgeable about investment structuring. Others in Yadav's office seemed to be clerical staff. Terry was apparently an investment banker working in his own capacity within the office, and he joined our discussions.

Things were progressing, but some gaps remained. Where was the money coming from?

'Nagendra Yadav is no big player, yet he was ready to sign a cheque for ₹700 crore. Edelweiss had said they couldn't lend more than ₹100 crore, and everyone knows Edelweiss. Neither of us had heard of Nagendra Yadav before. So who was financing him?' quipped Mayuresh.

Another point of irritation was the ex-banker rarely answered calls. Informally, we learnt he wasn't a long-term employee but was drafted for specific transactions. Yadav increasingly looked like a fixer, though we weren't sure. We waited to see if he would really secure the funds. The 1% hope remained strong.

After one meeting, Yadav gave us a formal sanction letter offering ₹700 crore but requiring a 5% processing fee—1% upfront.

'We cannot proceed without the fees. No one lends to an NPA. I am the only person in the market ready to lend to you, and if I'm taking this risk, can't you risk that little money?' he told us. '*Tu samajhta hai … mujhe aagey karche karne hai.* (You understand, I will be facing many expenses.) So that's why I'm asking this.'

His reasoning was sound, but we knew we could not afford the upfront fee. Having been stung once in the Hirani case, we were wary of putting in money. Though 1% seemed small, ₹7 crore was far beyond our means. Could we even consider this path? We asked to pay it at disbursement instead.

'You can't even generate 1%, and here I am trusting you with ₹700 crore. That means you're not creditworthy. What if there's a problem or shortfall? I'd be stuck. You can't even put 1% on the table?'

We had more meetings attempting to negotiate this gap. Mr Shetty was willing to take a punt but not beyond ₹1 crore. The gap was huge.

In one meeting, we were asked to wait while Yadav met other clients. The waiting room was full, and his staff seated us in a dead end corner of a passage. There, we noticed a pile of about twenty folders like ours, lying forgotten. Opening them, we saw they were untouched, filled with reports, bank statements and documents we had painstakingly compiled—just like he had asked.

Would our files suffer the same fate? This sight ignited our suspicions.

We reviewed our observations from the months visiting Yadav's office. It was well-maintained and spacious, with clerical staff filing papers. A lady sat in front of a computer, always on the same screen, her keyboard silent, never typing or switching tabs.

Everything was starting to seem suspicious.

Yadav claimed to be an NBFC, but we had never seen an analyst, compliance officer, monitoring team or legal officer—key roles in any legitimate NBFC. Yadav, too, displayed pictures with famous people prominently on his walls. The feeling of déjà vu weighed heavily upon us. Another scam?

By September 2021, the gaps in Yadav's story became glaring as our unanswered questions piled up. During the period between the second bid and September, we endured the harsh electricity power cut episode and encountered a few wannabe investors like Sanjay Aggarwal and Nagendra Yadav. Nothing had borne fruit.

We knew the Malpani Group remained the only serious contender and continued our engagement with them. Finally, the Malpanis sent a separate, convincing and concrete letter to the bankers stating their interest in bidding for Imagicaa at a certain number. This letter triggered a third auction in September 2021, and we fully disengaged from Narendra Yadav.

## More Scams and Shams

By now, having encountered so many scams and shams, we had grown more aware of the hallmarks of these scamsters. Still, it takes considerable learning to pinpoint them early on. The problem is that during such uncertain times, when so much is at stake, hope becomes a double-edged sword. You need that hope to keep moving forward, but the same hope can sometimes lead you into troubled waters.

Nevertheless, not everyone we met was a fraud. Some simply did not understand how a public company functioned, while others knew investors with money and were trying to fit a square peg into a round hole.

We once met a broker who walked in wearing a shiny black shirt and trousers—completely unlike what you'd expect from someone in finance. We listened to him and he connected us to someone with potential, but for various reasons, the deal never materialised. A few months later, he came back and said, 'Thank you for hearing me out and treating me respectfully. I don't usually get to speak to people like you.'

Throughout our journey to find a genuine investor, we met many people. I'd say 80% wanted to make a quick buck and were frauds, but we also came across many well-meaning individuals who clearly stood out with their frank assessment of what they brought to the table and how we could move forward.

## The Final Round(s)

The Malpani Group's offer letter was accepted as a bid in the third auction. By this time, BOBCAPS had actively driven consensus among the lenders, and we felt we were nearing the finish line. Yet by then, we should have realised that a simple, clear-cut path was not meant for us.

The auction was purposely kept non-binding because another complication surfaced as we navigated the complex issues of NPAs, NCLT and public limited companies. According to SEBI rules, if a public company signs a binding agreement, it must disclose it to the stock exchange. The banks were still debating their options. In February 2022, after many rounds of negotiation, the banks agreed in principle to the Malpanis' offer letter but added that the offer would be subject to a Swiss Challenge round.

The Swiss Challenge method is a tender/bid process where a private bidder makes a proposal to the lenders, who then invite other parties to match or improve upon the proposal. The original bidder retains the right to match the best counter offer.

This ordeal seemed never-ending. We had a genuine buyer, yet the banks insisted on one more round of auction. Why?

The stark truth is that valuing a project is difficult. Who can say definitively that what is offered today is a fair value relative to the banks' original investment years ago? Banks often prefer the NCLT route over auctions because it removes decision-making from their hands. It's easier for banks, but can be disastrous for companies like ours genuinely trying to resolve an NPA crisis.

Throughout the NPA and auction processes, transparency is paramount. Transparency is a frequently used term because bankers, subject to multiple audits, must maintain thorough paperwork and clear processes to demonstrate to seniors, auditors and boards of directors that everyone was given a fair chance and that the utmost transparency was observed. The Swiss Challenge was a means for bankers to showcase their intent to be transparent.

Of course, this was a blow to the Malpanis, who had waited patiently for so long. The banks acknowledged this and assured us that they were keeping the Malpani offer on the table and, should a better offer arise, they would first allow the Malpanis to match it.

Once again, we found ourselves hitting the road, searching for solutions that would satisfy both the lenders and us.

*Amigo Mantra #23: It ain't done till it's done.*

*Amigo Mantra #24: Never, never, never give up, and if you ever about to, just try once more, don't give up!*

# Thought #9: The Tricky Art of Valuation

We had our first valuation in 2018, right after we turned NPA. When a company turns NPA, many people—especially lenders—look at you with suspicion. They doubt your intentions and question the veracity of your claims about the lack of funds. Many promoters have scammed banks and creditors by claiming bankruptcy, so the initial reaction is to doubt and paint everyone with the same brush.

As CEO, Dhimant was treading a very delicate path and didn't want to give lenders any reason to mistrust our intentions. He was overly cautious during our initial valuation. Despite multiple requests from the valuers to share our views, he refrained and only provided data. He didn't want to unknowingly influence the valuation in any way.

Later, he realised this was a lost opportunity. A valuation has many elements, and Imagicaa was a complex case with no comparable model to guide the valuers. Unlike valuing a steel plant, sugar mill or manufacturing unit—where comparable entities exist—there was no precedent of this scale in India, especially for a theme park. Moreover, Imagicaa had survived for many years and earned a name in the market. Our business was operational thanks to all the efforts during tough times. It was not a failed business model. Complicating matters further, our loan of ₹1,020 crore was the largest for any entertainment or theme park project in the country.

Without comparable models, valuers needed deep industry and niche insights to properly appraise Imagicaa. Where would they get that? The primary source of insight was the company itself.

Appraising asset value for a project like ours is not a simple mathematical formula—such as taking asset cost, adding inflation or deducting depreciation. The concept of marketability runs through valuation. Realistically, valuation is a craft—it is not mere art or pure science.

The key question is: how much would someone be willing to pay for the company?

For banks, understanding this helped gauge auction recovery values or reasonable negotiation levels. Asset value is never fixed; it fluctuates depending on usage years, replacement costs, marketability, realisable value and distress value—affected by prevailing market conditions, asset management during resolution and other factors. Valuation agencies aim to pinpoint the right value for their client at a specific time.

Over five years, banks conducted multiple valuations. Although numbers were never officially shared, unofficial channels revealed a steady decline in valuation towards distress levels. One problem was that each year, banks would accumulate unpaid dues and thus the apparent 'outstanding' versus the recovery value would be bulging. On the other hand, rising bank provisions, indicating anticipated losses on recovery, helped narrow the gap. Provisions represent anticipated annual loss value due to NPAs; as provisions increase, banks' recovery expectations diminish.

The initial 2018 valuation was ₹1,100 crore. In 2019, this dropped to ₹950 crore, and by 2021 it was approximately ₹750 crore.

We also learnt that many valuers focus only on the asset itself, ignoring the business generating value or its sustainability.

When uncertain, they often take the safer route and value close to book value—roughly the purchase cost minus depreciation. This is a safe and lazy valuation; the figure is easily found on the balance sheet and adds little insight.

These numbers are indicative only. For example, when prime assets like Lavasa became NPAs, their valuation (liquidation value, to be sure) stood at around ₹4,000 crore, but the market would not pay that. Ultimately, bids were accepted at roughly ₹1,800 crore.

When a scamster like Murli Vaman appeared at the 2021 bank consortium meeting and readily agreed to the bankers' demand of ₹725 crore, he derailed our process by several months. Despite the auction failure and exposure of his scam, the banks clung to that 'fake' number—even though credible buyers like the Malpanis were ready with ₹575 crore, their patience was severely tested.

Numbers truly are sticky. Once banks latch on to a figure, they resist deviating significantly without revisiting the appropriateness of the original valuation. A multiplicity of bankers brought a wide range of thoughts, thereby further complicating matters, with competing views—some wanting what they could get, others holding out for more. There was no easy solution.

Numbers affect how people view you. Both high and low valuations can be disastrous. If the valuation is too high, banks resist settling for less—even if there are credible buyers waiting. What bothered us during the first valuation—and made us keep a distance from the process beyond providing data—was that a very low valuation could lead banks to question how the asset's value (i.e. the bank's primary security) deteriorated. This might prompt probes into whether sanctioned money was misused.

In hindsight, Dhimant's so-called 'error' of withholding market insights—but still sharing required data—had the unintended benefit of limiting scrutiny beyond valuation issues. Still, as we progressed, we realised that sharing some marketability data earlier might have prevented the initial valuation from being so high, and kept expectations on track.

Life became tricky as we constantly changed hats when switching between lender meetings (requiring pessimistic valuation views) and equity investor meetings (which demanded optimistic perspectives). After all, why would an investor commit without optimism?

Valuation is indeed a double-edged sword.

# 10

# Last-minute Callers

*'With him you are* aar ya paar.'

WE MET MANY BROKERS AND SO-CALLED FIXERS DURING OUR journey. Many tried to scam us, and some were clueless. Among them all, the one person we still remember with a big smile is Purshottam Patel, aka Puru Bhai (name changed).

Somewhere between our third auction and the Swiss Challenge, Puru Bhai was introduced to us by another broker called Pintu Valiya (name changed). Pintu had come to us through an unlikely connection—Ajay Kale, who was part of an agent chain that connected us to another lender/investor Vijay Shankar (name changed), with whom also there was an adventure of sorts few months back. Pintu had listened carefully to our deal and told us he had someone who could pull it off. Puru, he said, was a middleman and real estate broker operating in the plush areas of South Mumbai—Malabar Hill and Breach Candy.

'Puru Bhai works differently, but he is known to a couple of top-notch billionaires. If he is convinced, he will take up your case. With him, it's *aar ya paar* (do or die). The only problem is he talks a lot, and every morning and evening he sends you messages with Hanumanji pictures. You'll need to respond to them. Remember my instructions carefully.'

We received many caveats about Puru Patel before our first meeting, leaving us perplexed about what kind of person we would meet. After our varied encounters with brokers—expecting anything from free stays to payments for first meetings—merely responding to WhatsApp messages and listening to rambling talks didn't seem like too much. We barely registered this demand and agreed to the meeting, not realising that even three years after Imagicaa's resolution, we would still be receiving 'good morning' messages with Hanumanji pictures from Puru Bhai!

When Puru arrived, we were quite taken aback to see he was accompanied by a lady he introduced as his assistant. It was an odd pair: Puru was short and stout, looking like a Gujarati trader dressed in a heavily starched white shirt, with a very expressive face. The lady had bleached golden hair and a heavily made-up face, with make-up applied thickly. She never spoke during that meeting—or at any other meetings—and her role seemed to be limited to laughing at Puru's endless string of comments, which he passed off as jokes.

We began the discussion by explaining our predicament and what we had done so far to address it. We also informed him of the aborted deal with the billionaire investor and how it was scuppered due to land litigation.

'You guys have dealt with him … that makes it easier,' Puru Bhai said. He then quickly pulled out his phone and called the gentleman. We could not believe he had the private number of an investor known for his reclusive nature. Our first thought was that it was a bluff.

'*Main Imagicaa walon ke saath hoon*,' said Puru ('I am with the Imagicaa folks').

Within seconds, he was speaking animatedly on the phone in Hindi with the investor. On hearing that he was with us, the investor angrily told him not to proceed with us, saying we had 'eaten' his money. The bitter reaction was not entirely surprising, but we realised two things: first, that Puru Bhai had genuine access to this investor and likely knew others like him too; second, that we needed to work even harder at repaying the investor.

At the end of the meeting, Puru jotted down the total amount due to lenders and the settlement figure required to pay the banks on a piece of paper, then added his fees. 'I don't need any emails or printouts; this is my term sheet. *Meri chitthi hi kaafi hai*.'

He folded the paper into a smaller size and put it into his shirt pocket. It was truly a unique term sheet. Later, we learnt that he wasn't proficient in formal English and was unfamiliar with many financial terms, yet he was known among some of the biggest businessmen and apparently worked successfully primarily as a real estate broker. His confidence was sky-high, matched only by his earthy—and sometimes crude—sense of humour, and his firm belief that everyone and everything had a price.

'You've come to the right guy. Don't worry, I will take care of you.'

Dhimant immediately took offence to this attitude; it did not sit well with him at first. But Mayuresh was calmer, saying, 'He seems like a loose cannon, but he has top access. We can try. Worst case, we go back to square one.'

After the call with the billionaire investor, Puru connected us to another billionaire investor and a very large temple trust.

We had brief encounters with at least three options that Puru introduced as new opportunities.

None of these engagements worked out, and what we remember most from those meetings was how Puru would crack a bad joke, say '*Kay thaioo*,' laugh uproariously at his own feeble attempt, and then extend his hand as if expecting applause. He did this not only with us but also on the way to meetings with high-profile investors.

Puru Bhai never bothered with a façade, and though we could never fully fathom his manner of speaking, we recognised his genuine worth. We engaged with him for about two months. He was decent, definitely not a conman, and his involvement gave us a few key insights through brief brushes with billionaire investors, as well as countless happy memories of his unique conversational style and idiosyncrasies.

Puru always told Mayuresh with a chuckle not to stress, saying he would relieve him of his worries.

## The Waiting Game

Our NCLT case had been ongoing since 2018. By February 2022, the Malpanis had been the steadfast investors who stood by us through all the ups and downs. We were just waiting for the Swiss Challenge round to pass and for this long-drawn ordeal to end, when suddenly two more seemingly serious bidders emerged—without any solicitation from us.

'Our deal has been "in the market" for a long time now. We are technically a two-auction-old case!' scoffed Harshvardhan.

In February 2022, we were informed that an asset reconstruction company (ARC) was interested in bidding for Imagicaa. Typically, an ARC would buy loans at a cheaper value and work on turnaround through finding a suitable buyer at a profit through interest income or at a higher value. They reached out through a dealmaker specialising in hospitality—Harshvardhan Jani, a well-respected investment banker. We were surprised, since the ARC had never contacted us directly. We were also cautious not to jeopardise the Malpani negotiations. As a listed entity, when formally approached, we felt obligated to respond. Mayuresh was tasked with taking them on a site visit, as requested. It wasn't the best time to visit, since the park was still closed due to the third COVID-19 lockdown, and only the hotel was operational. Yet, as they insisted, we couldn't say no.

Two people came for the visit: a young man in a dapper suit, who turned out to be an investment banker, and a sprightly seventy-six-year-old gentleman named Verma. Verma revealed he would be investing personally alongside the ARC.

Verma had settled in the US years ago, owning several motels. He was impressed by Imagicaa and envisioned bringing major global players like Six Flags and Disney to the park. One memorable incident was when Verma initially refused to eat at our five-star hotel, whispering with a chuckle that fresh food is rare in such places. After my insistence, he relented and enjoyed the meal so much that he retracted his earlier remark.

Before leaving, he invited us to another meeting with the ARC head.

Strangely, the next meeting was held in a relatively run-down office in a famous commercial building in Nariman Point. Our discomfort must have been apparent because Verma explained that they wanted to keep the meeting under wraps until things were finalised, which was why they hadn't invited us to their main office, where analysts, lawyers and senior members worked.

In this meeting, we spoke with the ARC owner, who revealed they had originally learnt about us from an obstinate litigant claiming rights to the property—but whose demands had to be settled before any investor could proceed. After some time, the ARC lost interest due to the litigant's irrational behaviour, exorbitant demands and unpredictable approach, but had later reached out to us through mutual connections.

'I can drag the case for another twenty or twenty-five years—till that guy gets ready for his grave,' one of them told us.

They were confident of their clout and their ability to use it against the litigant if he tried any strategy. We could barely hide a smile hearing two old men—one seventy-six, the other close to eighty—discuss wearing someone out!

We left after reminding them that the auction window was in fifteen days, advising that they needed to conduct due diligence and arrange funds quickly.

Dhimant was still sceptical, but he attended one more meeting. Meanwhile, the ARC team met one or two lenders directly to gauge their position—as dealing with lenders is their full-time role. Funnily, they told us a couple of times that they would 'work things out' closer to the auction date.

With the auction date approaching, they still hadn't taken formal steps with the lenders. Upon their prompting, we took them to meet Mr Shetty. It was a good meeting. Verma again cited his associations with Disney, Six Flags and others, sharing his vision for the park. Yet Mr Shetty questioned the timing: why was this happening so late when the auction was imminent, especially since 'the entire world' knew about the asset on auction? It seemed they were either in no rush or did not grasp the seriousness of the situation.

Finally, with just five days left before the auction, Verma said he would call Goldman Sachs for financing and asked us to check if the banks would allow an extension, given the limited time remaining. This suggestion left us speechless. We definitely could not afford any more delays. When we said so, they tried to threaten us: 'If you try going with somebody else, we will build a bigger theme park across your property and bury you alive.'

It was a difficult conversation, but we had no intention of letting go of an existing opportunity to finally close our NPA journey on a vain hope that Verma and his ARC would produce a last-minute solution. These interactions left us puzzled about their true intentions and inexplicable arrogance.

Yes, they were a genuine party representing a large, established ARC, but why were they so slow to act?

Throughout, we had been transparent about auction dates and the Malpani offer, yet they treated it lightly and expected an extension. It was hard to understand what they really wanted.

## Perplexing Intent

When it rains, it pours.

We hadn't met any serious investors for a while—only scamsters and shams had crossed our path. But soon after Verma, another keen investor appeared. Pintu Waliya, the broker who introduced us to Puru Bhai, knocked again and introduced us to T.P. Sharma.

At our first meeting, we told him the Malpani deal was almost fixed and the banks would be conducting an auction soon. Despite this measured statement, T.P. Sharma was very keen on Imagicaa. He said he had to invest USD 200 million across two transactions: one was already locked in for another theme park in India, and Imagicaa would be the second. He said the other theme park had already committed, and if we came on board, he would find a way to invest USD 200 million for a very keen investor.

The way he confidently detailed the other theme park's investment made us reassess him, because he knew so many minute details—things that couldn't be faked or Googled. Plus, he said he was receiving a formal mandate from the other park and even offered to show us the document. His unsophisticated but frank approach prevented us from shutting the door on him.

We were intrigued and asked who the investors were. He was reluctant to say for now but promised to provide all documents and proof of funds. There was a conviction in him unseen in most of our previous meetings.

During our next meeting, T.P. Sharma showed the promised document from the other theme park outlining their funding needs. We called the CEO of the other park, who was struggling financially, to verify the claim; he confirmed meeting Sharma but smirked when we asked if Sharma could really invest. That was enough for us to remain doubtful.

Pintu Waliya wasn't ready to give up. He called Mayuresh every morning and evening, insisting Sharma had funds ready to invest. Upon Mayuresh's cross-questioning, Pintu said he believed in the funds because Sharma had recently invested in a Hyderabad-based company. To back the claim, he even disclosed the company's name and how much was paid to which creditor—a highly confidential detail that made their case more believable. Finally, he revealed the investor was based in California.

Pintu Valiya was persistent, but we had been burned so many times by fraudsters that we didn't want to engage with Sharma. Yet, our investment banker always advised keeping options open, because anyone can sneeze at the last moment. As company officials, we couldn't outright refuse proposals that might increase lender recovery; we couldn't eliminate prospects so easily.

We told him we couldn't act directly but suggested he approach the banks through the auction. If he had funds, he could park them then.

Later, Pintu strutted into meetings with a new swagger because he had become the owner of a company—only companies can bid in auctions. They had registered a company, but creating one from scratch and completing the KYC process required significant effort. They soon realised numerous legal requirements and document validations were necessary.

After a while, we heard they had recruited a retired banker to assist with documentation. They contacted lenders directly and downloaded previous bids and Swiss Challenge documents available to prospective investors.

Frankly, the effort they put into building a company before the Swiss Challenge was remarkable—working on dozens of documents like undertakings, NDAs and financial bids. This convinced us there might be a genuine investor behind it. But we wouldn't bet money on it.

Then they played the trump card—while everyone talked about ₹575 crore for the auction, they declared they'd pay ₹650 crore! The banks loved the number, and we feared a repeat of the Murli Vaman episode, where a scamster's inflated bid derailed the auction and set a new sticky number in the system.

If genuine, this offer would be great for the banks. But we had no proof and knew this was our last chance to beat the NCLT courts. We had distanced ourselves from them, though we heard of their relentless activity.

To enter the Swiss Challenge, a company had to deposit ₹15 crore. Sharma told the banks he couldn't provide the money but could give a bank guarantee. The banks agreed, following precedents.

This was one of the few times we felt truly anxious—helpless bystanders watching events unfold. The real danger of losing everything—Imagicaa and all we had fought for—was very real. We were so close to the finish line.

Until the penultimate day of the challenge, the guarantee did not arrive. Then Sharma told the banks there was a bank holiday in the US and asked for an extension.

The patient Malpanis were losing faith. When they learnt of Sharma's request, they were furious and warned the banks that any extension would cause them to withdraw their bid for good.

We started receiving frantic calls from banks asking if Sharma was authentic. We told them what we knew—which was nothing. We had no idea who their real investors were or who was backing the project financially. Why should bankers depend on our word to verify an investor's credibility? They deal with many NPA cases; this was our first and hopefully only time facing such a situation. It was a dicey position. Banks might suspect we were trying to sabotage the auction. We preferred to stay neutral and let the process play out—whether pearls or mud.

We understood the bankers' challenge. Decisions were collective, needing approval by higher-ups. They could be questioned for not waiting for a higher bid offering ₹75 crore more.

During this tense period, the Malpanis rightly insisted banks demand proof of funds or at least some cash deposit before allowing a third failed auction. 'The other party should at least put ₹15 crore on the table,' they said. The bankers managed to placate them, and an extension was granted.

Two more days went by—the guarantee still hadn't arrived.

To verify if Sharma could be weeded out, banks took emergency action by appointing an agency to assess proof of funds, reportedly spending a couple of lakhs on the investigation. Within a day, they received a report stating the fund or company Sharma cited had shut down long ago, though some old letters printed on their letterhead were still circulating.

Another fraud? Perhaps not.

Both Pintu and Sharma believed so strongly in that bogus fund house that they even put in their own money to establish a company. Were they scammers, or were they scammed?

## The End of Chaos ... and a New Beginning

There is a quote that goes like this: 'If you want to hear God laugh, tell Him your plans.' Throughout this entire journey, God must have laughed many times.

Calling it a 'tough' journey feels far too bland for the rollercoaster ride we endured. We navigated the tumultuous twists of financial turmoil, faced the looming shadows of insolvency and, at the very end, were left ragged—sitting on the edge of our seats, unsure what the next phone call might bring.

If our life were a movie, the two of us waiting for the final call from the banks would be the perfect cliffhanger. We can just picture it—two amigos sitting in a room, waiting for a call that would decide whether the battle they fought so hard to win was finally over. After all the negotiations and meetings with scores of people—many with nefarious intentions—there was nothing left for us to do but wait.

The fitting finale came when the Malpani Group won the Swiss Challenge and took over Imagicaa by paying ₹575 crore to the banks in June 2022. It was a unique transaction involving an ARC, change of management and ₹75 crore worth of equity to the lenders.

One year later, the banks were reaping higher profits as Imagicaa's share price soared, pushing its market capitalisation to a staggering ₹4,000 crore—almost fully recovering the principal outstanding across ten lending banks before the NPA designation. Ashutosh Maheshvari and Venkatesh from IMAP, Sanjeev Saraf and Kunal Doshi from BOBCAPS and Subodh Gupta from Edelweiss were the bankers who finally stitched this deal together.

Resilience, resurgence, transformation, perseverance and courage may serve as motivational buzzwords to some, but for us, they were the forces that shaped and grounded us throughout this journey. These words embodied our best days, and we learnt more from living them than from any motivational speech we have ever heard.

As we write this, there is a deep sense of relief that we triumphantly crossed the finish line within the time allotted. There is gratitude that it all came together as it did—with a friend by our side and a company showcasing the potential of the vision it was designed to create.

*Amigo Mantra #25: Hope for the best, plan for the worst.*

*Amigo Mantra #26: Live the moment, keep moving and be ready to seize another day.*

# Thought #10: Sustaining Investor Interest in Complex Deals

Since 2019, we had been in regular contact with the Malpani Group. Through the various ups and downs of failed auctions, fund house negotiations, lockdowns and encounters with scamsters and investors, we consistently sent them updates about the company and our activities.

We would update the Malpanis regularly—via WhatsApp, emails, and over coffee—because we believed it was crucial to keep sharing the narrative. There was a lot of misinformation circulating about us on WhatsApp and within financial circles. Our primary duty when engaging with authentic investors was to clear the cobwebs surrounding us and build faith through a transparent and forthright approach.

The Malpanis were incredibly patient throughout the entire deal. Had they not been so persevering, it is doubtful we would have reached an amicable conclusion with the lenders or emerged from this maze. The failure of the second auction, due to Murli's bragging, severely tested their patience because afterwards, bankers insisted on a higher value based on Murli's inflated number.

The Malpanis would spend more than five hours travelling from Sangamner for half-hour meetings with bankers who would often tell them, 'Why don't you increase your offer?' or recount a complex maze of processes—an auction, followed by appointing a process advisor, then a consortium meeting.

We deeply appreciated Jai Malpani, the young scion; Prashant Runwal, group CFO and a finance whiz with a photographic memory who led from the front; and the guidance of Rajesh Malpani and Manish Malpani. They saw the transaction through countless twists, months of disappointment and bureaucratic inertia. Most interested investors would have walked away by that point, convinced the deal was too complicated with too many processes to manage.

A significant advantage for the Malpanis was that they were already familiar with the park business, operating parks in Lonavala and Shirdi. This gave them a starting point—they began by understanding the competition, discovering that Imagicaa, with its vast infrastructure, offered a more integrated entertainment destination.

More than focusing on numbers, they took a deeper interest in the transaction by assessing the actual value of the business. Based on what they saw and their views on potential growth, they offered a more viable number to the banks with unquestionable credentials. Their offer was neither as low as some fund houses suggested—under the erroneous assumption that 'banks have no other option'—nor as inflated as the fanciful bids from conmen like Murli.

One question we're often asked is, 'Why did you look for other investors when you had one genuine investor?'

One of our advisors explained that since this was a sum of the parts (SOTP) transaction until the very end, and dealing with a large conglomerate involved their own internal decision processes, it was imperative to identify one or two suitable buyers in case any dropped out midway due to unforeseen reasons. The focus, we were advised, should be on completing the transaction rather than trying to constantly improve the deal. Those were wise words that guided us throughout the journey.

We knew the Malpanis were genuine investors, but for any transaction with banks to proceed smoothly, having another bid created a more genuine bidding atmosphere. We have also seen tenders and bids deferred or called off when only a single bidder participates.

It makes both bankers and the final investor feel they have secured a good deal—human nature values something more when someone else also wants it. It's a classic example of a cognitive bias.

# 11

# Learnings

AT NETWORKING AND SOCIAL EVENTS, WE ARE OFTEN ASKED when conversations turn to our NCLT experience, 'How did you manage to endure crisis after crisis for such a prolonged period?'

Going through a trying time is vastly different from reflecting on it afterwards. When you look back, it appears as a single, clear path leading you out of the woods into the light. But while you are walking that path, the problems remain unsolved, the way forward unclear and the final solutions merely incubating as possibilities. You don't know the path, nor whether it even leads to a solution.

Humans are biologically wired to have a fight, flight or freeze response when confronted with volatile environments, unpredictable events and constant stress. Yet, none of these three options proved helpful nor could they have guided Dhimant to firmer ground.

There were so many discussions with our family and friends where they urged us to update our CV because they had never experienced such turbulent times in their careers. Dhimant's father-in-law spent thirty-five years with one company. For him, and many family members and friends, his 'leap of faith decision' seemed quite foolhardy. Yet whenever he reached out, he received timely advice and nudges without judgement—or maybe we were just too busy to notice. Because neither of us tends to overthink and we feel at home in fluid and ambiguous situations, we kept going.

Going through a crisis is tough and you need a strong support system around you. Dhimant was fortunate that his wife, Toral, became a tower of strength during this difficult time. Her greatest gift was never doubting my decision to fight this battle or asking him to quit. She would check in occasionally just to ask if all was well. This belief was the X factor that allowed him to face other emergencies without fearing what his family might think. Her unwavering faith in the Almighty and ability to make do with the bare minimum inspired him greatly. Seeing her unshakeable belief gave him strength as he battled crisis after crisis.

Dhimant joined Imagicaa in June 2012. It has been a fabulous experience, and he personally connected deeply with the brand and the happiness it brings to people from all walks of life. It is very satisfying, and he has learnt a lot during this journey. Almost every one and a half years over the last thirteen years, he has taken on varied assignments and roles, which added spice and kept him engaged, never allowing boredom.

The great camaraderie we enjoyed as a team, the open and happy work culture, the purpose to create delightful memories for people and the opportunity to be associated with one of the most beautiful entertainment destinations and beloved brands—Imagicaa—is something we thank God for. We couldn't have asked for more.

For Mayuresh, the reasons and support systems had different dynamics. Looking back, he has been associated with the project from Day One. He still remembers the day Mr Shetty was exiting

Reliance Mediaworks Ltd and asked if he wanted to join his new venture—which included a Universal Studios or Disneyland kind of park. Mayuresh immediately said 'yes' without even asking about remuneration or role.

Since then, he has held the mantle of Imagicaa's 'oldest employee'. When Imagicaa got caught in the current situation, he felt morally bound to work towards pulling it out of trouble since he had experience in consortium loan dynamics, land litigation, IPOs and of interfacing with the government. His experience could be critical to the turnaround.

Fortunately, most of his family members are teachers, government employees or HR managers. They have no knowledge of the nitty-gritty of finance or insolvency, and thus no one advised him to seek greener, safer pastures. Mayuresh's wife Roshani, an Ayurvedic doctor, kept him going with her concoctions to boost immunity and combat stress.

The people most puzzled by his decision to stay with an NPA company were his MBA batchmates. After graduating from a premier B-school, most of them had clear growth trajectories that involved switching jobs before settling in stable MNCs. The alumni get-togethers often ended with him answering their curious questions about why he stayed with Imagicaa, and some batchmates, like Sameer Mansukhani, would light-heartedly poke him about the share price, which had dropped significantly, and ask him to make good his loss!

They would ask, 'What's the plan?' Mayuresh's usual answer was, 'No plan.' He found unlikely support in a dialogue from the Korean film *Parasite*, released around 2019, just as our situation deteriorated with the first auction and failed fund house talks:

> Ki-woo, you know what kind of plan never fails? No plan at all. No plan. You know why? If you make a plan, life never works out that way. Look around us, did these people

think, 'Let's all spend the night in a gym?' But look now, everyone's sleeping on the floor, us included. That's why people shouldn't make plans. With no plan, nothing can go wrong and if something spins out of control, it doesn't matter.

With such wacky mantras, we made light of situations that were otherwise demotivating and demeaning. That was simply how we rolled.

Throughout the crisis, we spent a great deal of time together, discussing our observations and lessons from the day. Even after the NCLT journey concluded, we sat down to introspect—to take stock of what went right, what we could have done better and what should have been avoided.

Over time, these discussions guided us towards actions and ways of working that could loosely be called our 'ideology for crisis navigation and resilience'.

What follows in the coming pages is not Googled gyan but authentic learnings that shaped us as profoundly as our circumstances shaped them. These insights formed the foundation of our actions, and we hope they help you navigate crises—no matter what shape or form they may take.

# 12

# The Reality X-ray

Every time a setback occurs, you need to recognise it for what it does to you, your company and your present situation. Hope needs to be powered by a method—that's the only way you can prepare for a comeback. Optimism is just one side of the coin. Simply believing optimistically in your future is of little help if you don't truly understand the reality of your situation.

## Take Action

Often, friends, mentors or concerned family members would ask us, 'What action are you taking? Do something at least.'

How do you know which step to take? And how can you be sure that the step you take will lead to the result you want? The simple answer is: you don't know. The outcome of your step often depends on another person's reaction. Yet, you have to take your step.

One thing that became apparent after we turned NPA was how some bankers treated us differently. As long as we paid all our dues, we were the blue-eyed boys. Once classified as NPA, their attitude changed markedly.

In one meeting with a newly transferred banker overseeing our account's recovery, the two of us hadn't made an appointment; we simply went to update him about our amicable resolution efforts. Entering his cabin, we explained the purpose of our visit, only to be rudely cut off. He pointed to an open box of almonds on his table—left by a previous visitor—and said, 'These are not for you.'

We were shocked by his incivility. It was a deliberate, crude display of his power over us. We held back our anger: the purpose we had come for was bigger than his provocations, and this wasn't the time for a retort.

Such behaviour was rare, and many bankers later commended us for our proactive cooperation in resolving the situation. Yet, had we allowed this negative reaction to deter us from taking action, we would have missed greater gains.

That's where Reality X-Rays help. The faster you recognise and accept the reality of your situation, the easier it becomes to decide your crucial next steps.

Understanding that we were no longer in our previous position—and that some would exploit this fact—flowed naturally from that realisation. Once you see this, it becomes easier to engage in ways befitting your higher goals.

An unflinching assessment of reality is essential because at the intersection of optimism and action lies the acceptance of your situation and the search for purposeful progress.

Being at the helm, we had to continuously process vast amounts of complex information, contradictory views and strong emotions. To do this well, we needed to keenly observe what was happening around us. To *see* reality for what it really was. We had no luxury of shying away from it, but we couldn't let it undermine our confidence or belief either.

Another example comes to mind. When we learnt of a pending GST refund from the government about a month or two before we turned NPA, we decided to pursue it and began internal documentation to highlight its importance to leadership. When we started pursuing the refund in August 2018, we didn't know if we'd succeed. We didn't know anyone who had done it before. Our business was fully operational, generating enough to keep the park running. We began the NPA battle thinking our business would support us—until it didn't. Finally, these efforts bore fruit during the bleak, COVID-induced shutdown, when Imagicaa closed and its income ceased.

At that time, the GST refund felt like a miracle. But the many steps taken toward that outcome reflected our understanding of reality: Imagicaa needed money, and we had to pursue every possible option offering even a glimmer of hope. In doing so, we not only helped ourselves but many other businesses awaiting government refunds.

We both believe in taking action grounded in an honest grasp of reality, rather than being overwhelmed by it. By doing so, one shifts from viewing challenges as roadblocks to seeing them as problems to be solved, step by step.

We never knew for certain if a step would lead to a final solution. But that's the beauty of steps—you don't know which one leads to success, but you know what you must do *now*. Mayuresh often recalls the tagline of one of his favourite whiskies: 'Keep Walking.'

That's all you need to do—and sometimes, that's *all* you can do.

## Know Your Purpose

Being aware of the reality involves two parts: understanding what is happening outside, and being conscious of your inner world—not being attached to titles or roles.

When Dhimant started working at Imagicaa, he joined as the retail head. Back then, very few believed retail would be a major differentiator or a strong pillar of our offering. He was hired just months before Imagicaa's opening, after someone else had declined the position post-offer. At work, he was asked to focus on the product and was given a minimal retail budget.

Imagicaa was at a stage of creating something entirely new for the Indian market. Everyone on the team was driven by the higher purpose of building a world-class entity—and he too was captivated by that vision. That was the very reason he joined. He saw it as a ripe time for creation and innovation and felt childlike excitement about the possibilities.

He was given a small team of two young MBA graduates, Jaideep and Vishal, whom he jokingly called Jai and Veeru because of their obvious teamwork. No task was too small or too big for us. We eagerly rolled up our sleeves and worked hard. Since we were experimenting with new retail ideas, he often ordered small quantities of goods. Sometimes, the cost of freight or tempo transportation outweighed the value of the goods themselves. The trusted team never hesitated to use their personal vehicles to pick up, load and unload cartons. When needed, he even grabbed a chisel and helped build my stall. Among us, there was no ego or shame in doing any work. The goal was to create something of quality that would resonate with our audience.

Likewise, when the two of us searched for investors or spoke to bankers and lawyers, we always pursued a higher purpose. Our goal was to free Imagicaa from the NPA crisis because we genuinely believed in the project's potential, not just emotionally but backed by solid numbers.

When Dhimant became joint CEO, he realised our finances were extremely tight. Although operational, we couldn't afford large marketing spends. We had to pay outstanding dues to creditors and vendors. We soon realised the only inventory we had to offer was park tickets and hotel stays. So, we resorted to the world's oldest currency—barter! With clear recognition that the priority was to streamline cash flows on a shoestring basis while figuring out other issues gradually.

We were mocked for resorting to barter; people thought we'd lost our minds because we were losing margins. Yet, Raveendra Singh, our marketing head, and we decided to proceed, offering tickets as payment to vendors. Some trade partners, like Tushar Gogri, stood by us during the worst times, trusting Imagicaa and its team. Through barter, we repaid their trust, allowing them to recover their advances and earn from ticket sales. Another aim was to ensure salaries were paid on time. Employees measure a company's health by timely and full salary payments, especially frontline workers. We managed this during financial crunches by advancing ticket sales.

Barter was unpopular among some team members, but it allowed vendors to recover money and employees to receive salaries reliably. The higher purpose was to arrest cash flow gaps and regularise the creditor cycle to manageable levels. Within one year and three months, we achieved this and stopped barter once creditor levels normalised.

The Reality X-Ray must be 360 degrees.

You need to consider everything—from your company to the people you meet and their stated reasons for engagement. Even talking to potential investors requires modifying your ask to match their priorities. Some investors look for growth, others for stability and some simply want a good investment opportunity. Here, too, a deep understanding of your reality and what you can deliver versus their needs is essential.

Understanding reality brought deeper clarity to our purpose:

| **Purpose** | **Action** |
|---|---|
| We had to keep the park operational because if our main asset was not maintained, then there would be no business left for anybody.<br>When COVID-19 struck and the park closed down, we had to work harder to ensure that the machinery, the rides and the general upkeep of the area was maintained despite the lack of adequate manpower. | We conducted weekly checks on the park. The maintenance staff were drastically reduced during COVID-19, yet our team ensured that some work on maintenance was done every day. Machines won't pass on COVID-19 to you and vice versa! |
| We wanted our teams to be taken care of because we were always conscious that Imagicaa was supporting many households. Many of those were in small villages where they didn't have other means of employment. | We decided on a sliding scale of pay cuts, with the leadership team taking a higher cut and the least for the junior-most workers with the hope to revert the cuts when the situation improve. |

| Purpose | Action |
|---|---|
| We realised that whoever comes in as an investor should be able to keep this amazing project running to its full potential. | We started communicating with the Malpanis in 2018 and kept in touch with them through the entire journey even as we spoke to other investors. There were so many misconceptions floating around about us that keeping a channel of communication open was very important to clarify doubts/ concerns and rumours. |

Many times, while seeking investors, a DGM from a lender bank in a consortium meeting slyly would ask, '*Resolution ke baad kya*? What about you, Mr Dhimant?'

Our impromptu response throughout was simple: 'Right now, we have gathered to resolve the immediate problem affecting the banks the most. Later, we will focus on our own challenges.'

One step at a time—and never forget to keep a thick skin and smile through it all.

# 13

# Convocraft Connections

Until Dhimant became joint CEO in 2017, he didn't fully comprehend the extent of the problems Imagicaa was facing. It was only when he began interacting with Mayuresh and accompanying him to meetings with our lender banks that he started to understand the severity of the cash crunch caused by enormous loans.

If, as a new CEO, he knew so little about our financial health despite being part of the leadership team for a long time, we realised most of our team was completely unaware. Our operations staff worked out of Khopoli, where Imagicaa is located, and these financial discussions were limited to a few members of the finance team.

Thus, after the first NCLT notice in 2018, we decided to inform everyone about the current situation so they could make informed decisions. The first meeting with the various department heads was certainly not easy, as many wore shocked and defeated expressions. Most of the senior members still remember that landmark day when we booked a conference room outside our office, and Mayuresh delivered a presentation that came like a bolt from the blue for most of them.

After that meeting, we began routinely updating the senior leadership on developments. We also told employees that if they wanted to leave, we wouldn't stop them—but we were staying and fighting.

Our optimism and hope came from the fact that Imagicaa was a good business—operational and self-sufficient. Perhaps that hope was communicated to senior leadership through our words and actions, which is why many stayed with us when we joined hands with the Malpani Group.

## Candour Basics

People often think that when a company faces a crisis, the CEO's role is to project optimism and confidence to avoid frightening the troops. That's true, but there is much more beneath the smile of projected confidence.

What we learnt from years of handling this crisis is that people seek community and safety; they look to their leaders for clarity and information. Honest and clear communication builds trust and confidence. Saying one thing while secretly believing something entirely different does not work, because people eventually pick up on manipulative verbal and non-verbal cues. Facing reality and understanding our purpose were the building blocks of candid communication.

Speaking with candour while keeping hope alive is a delicate balance. You cannot inspire hope if you don't believe in it yourself. Confidence starts within you. You cannot project confidence you don't possess. Each time you think about this, you return to facing reality as it is. Facing reality hurts, but it also lights the way forward—because it connects you with purpose and authentic conversations.

Our shared belief in Imagicaa and our purpose to lead it out of crisis helped us communicate candidly with senior leadership and staff. This authentic dialogue, across various meetings and employee levels, gave people hope that they could face the challenges ahead. It also resulted in minimal attrition, which turned out to be the X factor during these difficult years.

Shivajee for the park activities and government liasing and Raveendra Singh for business and marketing made a great team.

## Rebuilding Trust with Banks

Most bankers were surprised by how regularly we interacted with them. In fact, it wasn't just the bankers—our secured lenders entitled to the first payout—but also our operational and unsecured creditors who were taken aback by our consistent responsiveness. Along with Sitanshu (our operations head), we made it a point to answer every call from every creditor, even if all we had to report was: 'We're trying.'

Our purpose was never to hide but to find a solution, and that commitment drove every interaction with our creditors. Sitanshu's skill in managing creditor relationships was simply remarkable. His friendly demeanour and constant accessibility made his word highly credible. He also went out of his way to manage operations with negligible cash flow in the best possible manner.

Communicating with bankers is not easy. As an NPA company, you will be treated differently. Be prepared for that when you try to explain your business constraints. Above all, keep communicating.

### *Banks and anti-gravity channels*

As an NPA company, one must realise that the usual channels of communication with banks will change. Typically, company promoters and founders are accustomed to engaging with senior bank leaders—chairmen or managing directors. But once your company becomes an NPA, those connections become distant or closed, as understandably no bank leader wishes to be closely associated with an NPA company.

In such circumstances, building a rapport with bankers becomes crucial. However, no business school teaches you how to manage a company once it turns NPA. What processes are involved? What kinds of evaluations and actions can bankers take?

Companies need to understand that becoming an NPA is a process within banks comprising many distinct steps. Yes, assets can eventually be attached, but only after following due process.

Bankers often become wary of NPA companies because they see them as opponents. They rarely disclose planned actions or upcoming evaluations. Early on, we used to send emails to the bank MD regarding our case, which Mr Shetty found perplexing and somewhat unhelpful. We never received responses, though a couple of times, messages were redirected to the appropriate teams. At that stage, we were essentially shooting arrows in the dark. Mayuresh later explained the banks' anti-gravity style of operating.

Bankers operate through many hierarchical levels and departments. The bankers who sanctioned your loans are different from those handling recovery and resolution. Building trust takes time, and patience is essential.

The accounts manager creating your company's file is often at a lower rung, while decisions rest with a managing committee many levels above. This committee relies solely on the information in your file. That was why we made multiple bank visits—we wanted to ensure the right message was conveyed, and that account managers understood the nuances of our case.

For example, when negotiating a one-time settlement, we repeatedly told account managers that our promoter, Mr Shetty, was willing to exit the company to ensure its survival and a fair recovery for lenders. Banks often misinterpret such settlements as promoter funding to retain control, which could mean bigger haircuts. Consequently, many bankers avoided backing such proposals, afraid to stick their necks out. Our job was to continuously emphasise to various account managers across multiple lenders that our proposal was different.

We were often kept waiting for hours at banks, but we persevered, making it a point to meet with lead banks at least once every month and other lenders on rotation to keep them updated, even if there were no concrete developments.

The earlier example of a rude banker was not representative of all bankers—just one individual. Over time, as bankers observed our efforts and saw that we were confronting the issue head-on rather than running away, their trust in us grew.

Keeping communication channels open gives bankers a sense of security—they understand you're not avoiding responsibility. This builds a degree of trust. Once established, bankers begin sharing information about processes involved, enabling you to act and plan more effectively.

### *Everything is connected*

Building relationships with bankers also helped us with our lawyers. We would often ask accounts managers from some of our lender banks for updates or documentation. On one or two occasions, a banker would provide a status update by asking their junior staff to write a simple one-line note: 'This proposal is being reviewed.' A simple line like that could bring immense comfort in court and help us buy another day.

Maintaining conversation and openness is challenging when things are not unfolding as you envisioned. It is a blow to the ego to admit you are not in the exalted position you once imagined. But facing reality is the first step towards creating candid conversations with your lenders, and that is the foundation of a good relationship.

### Investing in Experience

If we had to handle this entire crisis by ourselves, we would not have found success. This journey made us realise the importance of certain people and roles, among which the investment banker's role stood out.

Ashutosh Maheshwari of IMAP was our investment banker, and we can confidently say that many breakthroughs happened because of his keen understanding of the situation and his dispassionate approach to addressing pain points. Surprisingly, this relationship began with a cold call to Mayuresh from one of IMAP's senior members, Venkatesh, and gradually grew into one built on deep trust and confidence.

Unlike most investment bankers who arrive with a large team, Ashutosh is a one-man show, supported by a small, close-knit backend team. During this journey, we also worked closely with Anand Desai, Ashish Pahariya and Soham Mukherjee of DSK Legal from our side, as well as Milind Jha of Link Legal, who helped shepherd this transaction with patience and calm to ensure it went as smoothly as possible. Cutting through noise and ego is vital in such transactions, and we witnessed their simplicity and humility firsthand.

When we initiated talks with the Malpani Group, we had built upon the plan to divide the business into three parts: the hotel, the amusement park and the land. We had an investor interested in the land, were in talks with a giant conglomerate for the hotel and were engaging with the Malpani Group for the park business. We needed an investment banker to help piece these three buyers together because, as company representatives, neither of us could be the dealmaker. Additionally, as Imagicaa was designed as an integrated amusement park, dividing it was complex.

Over the years, Ashutosh handled some of the most complicated situations with bidders, financial structuring challenges and senior banking meetings. While many would focus on how to structure this complex deal, Ashutosh would propose out-of-the-box ideas. When new ideas were met with scepticism about regulatory approval, Ashutosh would win people over with his encyclopaedic knowledge, mentioning how ABC Corporate had executed a similar structure last month or how RBI had permitted a certain structure for XYZ Corporate.

His experience, skill and objectivity proved decisive for us numerous times, and others recognised his expertise as well. In fact, Ashutosh was part of our team during the Malpani deal. After its completion, the Malpanis welcomed him into their team for further discussions.

There is no substitute for experience and expertise, and you need both when you are in a tight spot.

# 14

# Inventing Solutions

You never know what inspires you or what gives you the motivation to keep trying when everyone around you has given up.

In the early days of the crisis, we decided to focus on each ball in play. The scoreboard was not in our vision, but the ball was in our hands. So, we chose not to spend time worrying about things that might never happen.

The fact was, we were facing an unprecedented crisis. There was the NPA, the NCLT process and COVID-19 . The banks had never dealt with a case like ours, so they had no precedent for asset valuation or business understanding. Often, there were so many possibilities that speculating on what could or might happen felt like a waste of time.

'Hope for the best, prepare for the worst,' became our motto.

Many people assume that once an NCLT application is filed, it's only a matter of time before all is lost. But as we interacted with all stakeholders, we realised numerous technicalities had to be addressed first. So our focus remained on taking each day and each step as it came.

In a crisis defined by uncertainty, focusing on each day and each step helps avoid overreacting or jumping to conclusions just to ease discomfort. You begin to find opportunities to work with deliberate calm and optimism. Carrying the burden of the outcome too early can break your spirit before you reach the end. Thus, becoming overly fixated or obsessed with the outcome is counterproductive. It's important to enjoy the journey and keep your cool.

Maybe it's a mindset. Dhimant tends not to overanalyse or cling to one way of doing things, which helps him improvise. Often, he is quick to criticise his own suggestions once a better idea comes from others.

On the other hand, Mayuresh does overanalyse but perseveres, constantly thinking of ways out. His thorough research and archiving have often helped us unravel hidden complexities in negotiations.

## The Art of Asking

Perhaps because of a specific mindset or a particular faith in humanity, but we have never hesitated to ask—the worst anyone can do is say no. A no won't harm us. At worst, someone will say something won't work; at best, it might open a new way to find a solution.

Dhimant had a big advantage: unlike Mayuresh, he wasn't bound by past assumptions about working with bankers. Mayuresh had worked as an investment banker and been part of Imagicaa's funding phase, interacting with bankers almost weekly. This made him think he knew what bankers 'would' or 'would not' do, and he often avoided asking where he knew the answer would be a no. Dhimant, on the other hand, would boldly plead his case. This helped us on many an occasion. One notable instance was when we asked for the return of the cutback as Imagicaa was shut due to COVID-19.

Dhimant's rationale was, 'Use me, buddy. I'm the new kid on the block for banks.' This no-baggage approach was hard for Mayuresh initially, but when he saw the open windows that were hidden in plain sight, he began to believe in it too.

What also helped Dhimant was that, as a new CEO, he could honestly claim no knowledge of the loans taken before he joined. That allowed him to shift the conversation from 'What happened?' to 'What needs to be done to move ahead?'

Asking helps. You never know the answer until you ask. Often, bankers themselves were intrigued by the question: will this work? Can this work? They could always say no, but asking made them pause and think.

This kind of *asking* came from a deep sense of belief. We had done no wrong. We wanted to repay our loans, but to do that, we had to survive.

We also realised the importance of saying 'I don't know'. It is a great ego-shedder because as CEO, you're expected to know everything, which is impossible. Saying 'I don't know' invites others to share ideas. Once you listen, you may hear suggestions that help you find a better way. Unlimited one-liners and quotes during our journey—such as, 'Fortune favours the prepared mind'; ' Everyone is the same in the bathhouse'; 'Sweat in peace, bleed less in war'—kept coming at regular intervals. Two memorable ones were: 'Hope for the best but plan for the worst' and 'Why fear and worry about consequences when you have taken the risk'.

After months of the pandemic shutdown, most businesses reopened, but amusement parks remained closed for over a year. In desperation and hope, we began writing emails to Mantralaya and the chief minister asking for help. We followed up weekly.

We found inspiration in the movie *Shawshank Redemption*. One of the most moving scenes was when Andy Dufresne finally receives a response after writing weekly letters for six years requesting books and library materials for the prison. The authorities ended their letter with, 'Please stop sending us letters.'

Andy's response was, 'Now I will write two letters a week instead of one.'

We sent the first email on 26 April 2020 and continued until 2 May 2021. The emails began with bold caps: HELP PLEASE HELP. We made a case for Imagicaa, explaining we had no income and a staff of more than 1,500. We received very few responses, but we kept writing and sending those emails. We must have sent around twenty-five to thirty, confident someone had read them.

## The Pandemic Brain

Going through an NPA phase was challenging, but the company was still EBITDA positive. The biggest hurdle during this journey came when COVID-19 hit. Morale plummeted. With no income from the park, employees were stuck at home, bombarded with painful and devastating news about the pandemic. We soon started team calls, not only to explore ways to market or generate income, but mainly to maintain connection. These calls became a vital way for us to touch base, exchange jokes and pleasantries, share fears and concerns and brainstorm ideas together. Keeping all of us away from 'idle-mind situation' was very essential, we thought.

During the pandemic, we still travelled to Mantralaya or Khopoli, conducting team calls inside the car. On one such ride, Mayuresh suggested, 'Why don't we have an open ticket like some airlines?' That was a brainwave.

One challenge in our business was that no one knew *when* they would be able to visit the park—the plan was always for 'someday'. Which day would that be? How do you keep people motivated and engaged? How do you plan for that uncertainty?

Mayuresh's idea sparked our team to launch an Independence Day 2021 offer: an eye-watering 74% discount on tickets, valid for use within a year of the park reopening. It was a massive hit that generated over ₹1.3 crore in cash flow, keeping the Imagicaa lamp burning bright. Encouraged by that success, we ran more campaigns that brought in ₹7 crore during COVID-19.

To keep the buzz around Imagicaa alive, we created an online activity called *Quarantivities*, which spread joy during the lonely and desolate quarantine period. Skilled professionals—chefs, character illustrators, dancers and more—conducted free online training sessions that people could register for. These activities got people involved and engaged.

We also launched the first gratitude campaign for COVID-19 warriors, thanking doctors and nurses. They were invited to register online for a free park visit. Viewers soon started recording and sharing videos saying, 'I love Imagicaa' and 'I miss Imagicaa'. What started as marketing evolved into building a community. Sometimes, people messaged us asking for oxygen cylinders, and we did our best to arrange them. We distributed leftover provisions from the park to nearby villages.

We also realised we relied heavily on external software for park ticketing and online bookings, so we began converting these functions into an internal system. That saved us money in the long run and built in-house capabilities.

Working on these ideas kept the team busy and infused a critical dose of hope and positivity when everything was shut down. It kept everyone focused on developing good ideas for the brand. There is always so much to do, and any action is better than sitting and moping.

# Conclusion

*Never give up.*

That's the answer to the question we started with: how did you keep bouncing back after each disappointment and scam?

Never giving up is as much about hope as it is about overcoming doubt and accepting reality for what it is and what it can become. It's about not letting that flame diminish because you believe this is a fight worth fighting.

Resilience is often said to stem from an optimistic nature. Yet unfettered optimism can distort reality. There is an anecdote in the *Harvard Business Review* titled 'Managing through a Downturn' that discusses Jim Collins, author of *Good to Great*. While researching resilient companies, Collins suspected they were filled with optimistic people. So, he asked Admiral Jim Stockdale, who was held prisoner by the Viet Cong for eight years, for his view on resilience.

*Collins: Who didn't make it out of the camps?*

*Admiral Stockdale: Oh, that's easy. It was the optimists. They were the ones who said we were going to be out by Christmas. And then they said we'd be out by Easter and then out by Fourth of July and out by Thanksgiving and then it was Christmas again. You know, I think they all died of broken hearts.*

Never giving up is not just optimism. It means facing reality, taking action, finding your purpose and persevering until the very last moment, because you never know where things might go right.

We kept meeting new investors even after encountering scamsters. We kept going to banks even when bankers grew cold toward us. We kept talking to our employees and operational lenders because we had to keep our company running despite everything. We followed the 1% Hope principle. And that 1% delivered at the end.

# Acknowledgements

Many of our associates, such as vendors, lawyers, advisors, mentors, colleagues and family members, deserve a thank you from the bottom of our hearts for being instrumental at various critical junctures and making it happen. We have attempted to list the names to the best of our abilities below.

**Vishal Kamat** (*business leader / industry face*): Part of a legendary family, Vishal is a highly energetic person who thinks on feet and is always available for guidance. He also comes with a great network.

**Ashutosh Maheshvari** (*investment banker*): A one-man army, Ashutosh has razor-sharp brilliance, incisive understanding of business situations and is armed with a beautiful mind for complex problems.

**Sanjay Asher** (*senior lawyer and firm partner*): Sanjay is a highly approachable luminary, a wonderful gentleman and a lawyer with a golden heart. We couldn't have got anyone better in our crisis.

**Sanjeev Saraf** (*investment banker / process advisor*): Sanjeev interacted with us in various avatars and was always supportive and positive. In his second avatar, he seemed destined to be part of the solution.

**Samir Shah and Jigar Kavaiya** (*investor relations*): Samir advised us in various situations, and his ability to comprehend the situation was impeccable, his quick wit and one-line solutions were profound and thought-provoking. Jigar, his able lieutenant, was ever-positive in his approach and went out of his way to make things work.

**Abhishek Rastogi** (*senior legal counsel*): Abhishek was the man who turned the tide for us in the worst situation. He is fearless and passionate, with amazingly sharp wit, great ability to see beyond the normal and make things happen.

**Prateek Seksaria** (*senior legal counsel*): With his remarkable ability to interpret and understand the situation, Prateek was simply excellent in his approach and on the battleground. We were blessed to have him by our side.

**Kiran Chonkar** (*process advisor*): The first rounds of auction would have gone poorly but for his dogged approach. Kiran comes with nuggets of wisdom for all sides and always has the end goal in sight. He is never afraid to speak his mind.

**Ameet Naik** (*senior lawyer and firm partner*): Ameet leads a large firm, but tracks of all case dynamics like a hawk. He was personally invested in our case. His awareness of the market and his network are impeccable.

**Ashish Pahariya** (*senior lawyer*): Ashish is a cool and calm lawyer who will put you at ease and give you thoughtful, practical solutions that get your work done.

**Simone Reis and Rajesh Simhan** (*legal experts*): Both Simone and Rajesh are technical experts in legal and forex stuctures and regulations. Their friendly guidance was invaluable at more than one juncture.

**Kunal Doshi** (*process advisor*): Kunal is a young professional geared to be on a fast track. A great improviser, he is able to balance situations based on the tensions between people. Handling different levels of public sector bankers is no mean task, and he did it smoothly.

**S. Venkatesh** (*investment banker*): An experienced professional, Venkatesh comes with a logical question bank, and he delivers his answers with calm and a bit of sarcasm too!

**Tushar Gogri** (*business associate*): Tushar supported us against all odds, believed in Imagicaa more than most and helped us almost as a hand of God in extremely vulnerable times! He was ably supported by Abhishek Sinha, who could think out of the box and added value to our journey!

**Komal Khushalani** (*law firm associate*): A diligent lawyer with a penchant for detailing and persuasion, Komal has a calming presence even in chaotic times that helped us sail through rough waters.

**Shadab Jan** (*law firm associate*): Shadab is an ambitious young lawyer who works with enthusiasm and sincerity. He was on the ground on many occasions.

**Sanjay Jain and Piyush Chande** (*Aditya Birla ARC*): Sanjay and Piyush understood the transaction and navigated the technicalities in a very professional manner.

**Rohit Mehta, Amol Bhutada and Rahul Toshniwal** (*Edelweiss*): Rohit, Amol and Rahul explained to us the concept of 'seasoning of account' and the nitty-gritties of a resolution plan. They handled our account at an early stage.

**Malpani Executives and Advisors:**

**Prashant Runwal and Prafulla Khinvasara:** These were the 'Awesome Twosome' of the Malpani Group whom we coordinated with through this phase of resolution. They were always available and worked as a team to make things happen! Meticulousness and detailing are hallmarks of these gentlemen.

**Gopal Agrawal, Subodh Gupta and Priti Sahay** (*Edelweiss*): Gopal, Subodh and Priti were enthusiastic and committed to make the transaction happen. They tried their best to balance all sides.

**Milind Jha and Aditya Bhardwaj** (*Link Legal*): Calm and composed in every discussion, Milind and Aditya made sure the transactions were appropriately structured and executed.

**Our Colleagues**

**Sitanshu Satapathy** (*Accounts / Operations*): Adept at people management with an uncanny ability to find solutions despite odds, Sitanshu fulfilled all the roles that we didn't know whom to assign. Clearly our Man Friday!

**Col. Ashutosh Kale** (*Jt CEO / Operations*): A former member of the Armed Forces and champion of the security perimeter for the park, Col. Kale's one-liners and military strategies both got deployed to full effect!

**Balanand Anand** (*Engineering*): Detailed and meticulous at tasks and a perfectionist to the core, Anand was a key signatory in corporate affairs. He trusted the rest of us in non-engineering matters.

**Shivajee Sharma** (*Operations*): A charismatic leader with great initiative to make things happen and the vice chair of the industry association IAAPI, Shivajee led from the front in keeping the system moving during the COVID-19 lockdown.

**Raveendra Singh** (*Marketing*): Raveendra is highly intellectual and logical in his marketing assessment and always to the point. With immense patience, he innovated and ensured the brand was seen in its true light.

**Veeraj Shenoy** (*F&B*): Veeraj is a very creative business head. He keeps one eye on the guest experience and the other on the costs.

**Manasvi Wani** (*Infrastructure / Civil*): A detail-oriented person, and amazing at getting things done at the ground level, Manasvi handled the infrastructure of the park through and through with patience and despite the complications of the local ecosystem.

**Mahesh Gaikwad** (*Scenic*): A soft-spoken person with a high level of creativity and execution skills, Mahesh's team's efforts blunted the effect of lockdown on the park upkeep and added life to the destination.

**Shibu Nair** (*Operations*): Great at managing events and mobilising resources and thorough with overall operations, Shibu was always available and handled tough times with a smile. He was Mr Dependable.

**Arvind Kamalia** (*Finance*): A one of a kind person, Arvind zealously saved every paisa, was meticulous in documentation and a master of ceremonies when it comes to organising, be it a bank visit, team outing or a Diwali pooja!

**Vishal Sampat** (*Retail*): *A* complete charmer with infectious energy, Vishal handled situations and importantly Dhimant's tantrums as the retail head.

**Naresh Bisht** (*Engineering*): Innovative and always keen to find Indigenous ways of doing things, Naresh was a key member in kick-starting rides!

**Pradeep Suryawanshi** (*Liason / Legal*): The man from Baramati, whom we jocularly called 'Singham', Pradeep wielded his clout and tact across the local offices and gram panchayats and got many an important approval for the parks and hotel.

**Ravindra Kulkarni and Amit Patil** (*Liaison*): Ravindra and Amit showed unbelievable energy and exceptional liaising skills. They handled various challenges with a smile and worked immensely to reopen the park post-COVID.

**Amarnath Mhamane**: This book would be incomplete without a BIG credit to Amarnath. In fact, many adventures started from the various leads that he brought to the table. A dedicated team member, he had unbelievable confidence and faith that things would work out positively in the end.

**Sachin Malhotra**: Strong and a very methodical professional, Sachin rose to the occasion during COVID-19 and took a bold call to operate the hotel with a most nimble approach. He led from the front at the critical and sensitive phase of reopening the hotel post-COVID.

## Team Members on this Rollercoaster:

**Marketing**: Hasmukh Gorava, Prateek Panchal, Sneha Raut, Sanchita Attawar, Shamian Waghmare

**Sales**: Dhiraj Bargal, Dipesh Gupta, Linus Gonsalves, Varun Pawar, Pankaj Jha, Sameer Ghag, Sushil Mistry

**Creative**: Ravindra Parab, Koyal Maji, Viraj Khadke, Shadab and Rashmi Padyar

**Retail**: Sandeep Ramane , Arshad Shaikh, Maninder Singh, Nitin Shewale, Mahendra Kurgatkar, Ratnesh Tiwari, Aadam Shaikh, Nilesh Kamble, Ganesh Adasul, Ganesh Lokhande, Dinesh Haldankar

**F&B**: Chethan Gowda, Chef Irrfan, Debabrata Pradhan, Yogesh Mhatre, Rajkiran Jadhav, Shekhar Thakur, Mahaveer Prasad, Deepak Sonawane, Lenin Kumar

**Procurement**: Varghese Philip, Janardhan Thakur, Nandan Ture, Deepali, Ganesh Babar

**IT**: Lakshmana Vadaga, Kamlesh Ghate, Ganesh Khatri, Awadhesh Singh, Ritwik Shaman, Narendra Joshi

**Engineering**: Sharad Swaroop, Vasant Anandrao, Yogesh Tiwarri, Dipak Patil, Sanjay Mhatre, Hemant Khaire, Prashant Gade, Viswas, Ikram, Pritam Kamble, Purshottam Solanki (Bunty), Mangal Sakpal, Vishawas Raut, Ganesh Junnarkar

**Operations, Admins, Safety & Security, Scenic**: Mahesh Bansode, Biswaroop Chaudhary, Nachiket Kulkarni, Aditi More, Priyanka Karnuk, Jagdish Patil, Zanda Singh, Hemant Musale, Yuvraj Tandel, Rahul Shirke, Dr Swapna, Anita Sharma, Dnyanoba Kamble, Sameer Nagaonkar, Vitthal

**F&A**: Mahadev Aglave, Khelan Shah, Sarafat Shaikh, Sadanand Gaikwad, Amol Budar, Dattaprasad Vaidya, Santosh Kamble

**Novotel Imagicaa**: Anil Chavan, Kedarnath Biswal, Govind Belekar and Waseem Karbelekar

## On the Book:

To our wonderful ghostwriter, who helped us pen down all of the above adventures, put everything down in a structured manner and had loads of patience in handling our wisecracks through this process; we truly appreciate your efforts from the bottom of our hearts.

To our friends Bakul Nair, Anirudh Kalia, Srividya Kedar, Dr Swapna Pradhan and Ajit Uncle, who spared precious time to go through the sketchy version and shared their valuable feedback which helped us improve.

To Uncle Gajendra Kore, who encouraged us at the very start to get writing and shared precious insights as a writer himself.

To all those wonderful people who requested anonymity due to the roles they play, as they read these passages with a hidden smile: we hope they get heartfelt thanks from the two amigos!